"The Criminal Justice System is being hamstrung by lefty human rights lawyers and other do-gooders."
Boris Johnson (when) Prime Minister

"Lefty lawyers, 'enemies of the people'…
upholding the law is a crime in some eyes."
Charles Falconer, former Lord Chancellor, Guardian

"We should all be thinking of effective ways to counter the nonsensical insult that disgraceful 'lefty lawyers' are standing in the way of a heroic government."
Jonathan Goldsmith, President, Law Society

Lefty Lawyer

ISBN 978-1-914603-55-6 (Paperback)
ISBN 978-1-914603-56-3 (EPUB ebook)
ISBN 978-1-914603-57-0 (PDF ebook)

Published 2025 by Waterside Press Ltd
www.WatersidePress.co.uk

A catalogue record for this book can be
obtained from the British Library.

Ebook *Lefty Lawyer* is available as an ebook
including through library models.

Publisher's note: The views and opinions
in this book are those of the author
entirely. Readers should draw their own
conclusions, concerning which the possibility
of alternative narratives, descriptions and
interpretations should be borne in mind.

Printed and bound by Short Run Press.

Lefty Lawyer
Speaking Truth to Power

Pauline Campbell

✖ **WATERSIDE** PRESS

To the real heroes of this book, Waldes and Desseline, my Mum and Dad, and those like them from the Windrush Generation, who came here all those years ago to give me and my generation the chance of a better life.

Contents

Acknowledgements

My appreciation should begin with Dad and Mum, who left the warm sun of Jamaica to make a home in a country that welcomed them with signs: "No Blacks, No Dogs, No Irish." Who, despite all the racism they experienced, stayed to give me and my siblings the hope of a better life. Thank you for giving me the grounding needed to embrace my Jamaican culture, alongside the British girl in me that was equally important, by inviting my white friends into our home and never making them feel unwelcome despite all the inequality that had taken hold of your lives.

Thank you to my sisters and brothers, with whom I am proud to share such a strong bond, including the highs, lows, and ups and downs on this incredible journey. And to my husband, Everton, whose strength and resilience has kept me strong and focused.

I have to thank my previous manager, Vicky Addai-Diawuo, who sadly is no longer with us, who agreed to allow me to continue working while undertaking a full-time law degree and encouraged me as I drove between work and university for three years. I am further indebted to my lecturers at the university, who listened to my moans and groans and kept me on target in securing my law degree, and to those amazing friends, Judy Cato, Lorraine, and Petula Dowe, who never gave up on me, despite my many absences from various social events.

Further thanks are owed to my publicist, Robin Heller, President of Athena Advisors, who took me on as a client and helped to tap into my potential by opening the doors to educational speaking events and, significantly, introduced me to the highly talented Laetitia Pancrazi, who read my manuscript and whose invaluable advice and constructive detailed feedback pushed me to higher levels within my writing, that led me to the juncture that resulted in meeting Bryan Gibson, of Waterside Press, whose belief in my work has resulted in *Lefty Lawyer* being published.

Thank you to Trevor Sterling, a legal giant, one of just 90 black partners in the UK, and senior partner of Moore Barlow, who invited me as a guest on his fantastic podcast to inspire people not just to climb the ladder of success but to be the ladder. Thank you for your continued support and for being an all-around nice guy.

Thank you to my good friend, renowned actor, and CEO of the Justice-4Windrush charity, Colin McFarlane, who has placed his faith in me to be the pro bono lawyer for this important organization. Colin's powerful presence, strength, and tenacity in fighting for the rights of those impacted by the Windrush Scandal are testaments to him.

It would be impossible to thank everyone by name, but this is a call out to all my work colleagues who continue to support every school, college, university, podcast, and legal firm that has invited me to speak. To my social media followers who share my messages in the fight for equality and to the Windrush Generation still fighting for compensation, thank you for trusting me and allowing me to help you through the trauma you suffered.

Pauline Campbell
January 2025

About the author

Told at school that she was 'not A-Level material,' Pauline Campbell began training as a solicitor in her early 30s. After qualifying at age 41, she worked for Hounslow Council, then moved to Hackney Council as a lawyer, after three years securing a senior role, before moving to Waltham Forest, where she holds the position of Principal Lawyer.

The daughter of Windrush Generation parents who came to England from Jamaica in the 1960s, she trained in the magistrates' courts in Kent before becoming a senior lawyer with Waltham Forest Council.

A fearless advocate and voice for those affected by the Windrush Scandal, she has provided pro bono advice to over 100 of its victims. She is chair and a trustee of the charity Justice4Windrush, and legal adviser and advocate for applicants making claims via the Windrush Compensation Scheme. A creator of 'safe space clinics' in the work place, she is chair of Waltham Forest's Race Equality Network.

In 2024 Pauline Campbell was one of just five solicitors chosen from nearly 500 participants recognised by the Law Society as Legal Heroes due to 'the impact of their work beyond the bounds of their profession that made a profound and lasting impact on the lives of others and society.'

Her novel *A Touch of Templeton* (under the pen name P E Campbell), was published by Grosvenor House in 2015 and her previous non-fiction book *Rice, Peas and Fish and Chips* by Twenty-Seven in 2021. More widely, she has used accounts of the early academic discouragement she received to give hope, encouragement and support to the less privileged, the vulnerable those in adversity and 'late starters' in particular.

About the author of the Foreword

Trevor D Sterling is a multi-award-winning major trauma solicitor and the Senior Partner at Moore Barlow. In 2021 he was elected to that position becoming the first Black Senior Partner in a Top 100 UK law firm. He has represented clients in many notable and high-profile cases. He ranked No. 1 LinkedIn Leader in 2024 and received an Association of Jamaica National Hero Award (UK) in the same year. He is Chair of the Mary Seacole Trust, a charity which promotes racial equality.

Foreword

Trevor Sterling

In the cold winter of 1959, my parents arrived in the UK from Jamaica. Like many before them, their arrival was effectively on invitation to help build a better Britain and, from their perspective, for them to provide a better future for their loved ones.

They were part of the Windrush Generation and what was to follow was the birth of a generation of Windrush descendants, who would unwittingly be faced with a British system riddled with inequality. To prosper, their children needed to develop the skills to navigate a society filled with a gravitational pull to hold them down.

Having left school at 17 and by pure luck, I secured a position for a law firm delivering legal papers to barristers as an 'outdoor clerk' and nearly 40 years later I am able to look back over an illustrious career in which I made history. Becoming the first Black Senior Partner of a top 100 UK law firm. In 2024, I began a podcast series called "U-triumph", putting into effect my mantra: "Don't just aspire to climb the ladder; Be the ladder". My aim was to share inspirational stories of those who had overcome societal challenges and then become the ladder by giving back.

Top of my list of interviewees for my podcasts was Pauline Campbell. I had learned of her remarkable journey having read her book *Rice and Peas and Fish and Chips*, a work which resonated deeply. Pauline had brilliantly written her book with a combination of empirical experience and extensive research, creating a navigational journal for the next generation.

When asked to write this Foreword for *Lefty Lawyer*, I did not hesitate. Pauline skilfully adds embroidery to her earlier work, outlining how she navigated societal challenges to pursue a career in law, eventually qualifying as a solicitor aged 41. Having qualified, one key driver from thereon was her desire to not simply climb the ladder but to fulfil her purpose and make a difference. She has deftly recounted her experiences which will resonate with many, how these fuelled her to not only challenge herself to become an excellent lawyer but to be a champion for others, particularly tackling racial inequality and supporting victims of the Windrush Scandal.

One can only draw inspiration and know-how from her achievements. Pauline fills me with admiration as to how she has had, and continues to have, a huge impact on societal inequalities. Her experiences provide not just the armour but the sword to address racial inequality, particularly in respect of the black community.

If there is one thing that Pauline has not changed, it is how she achieved what she has achieved whilst remaining her authentic self. I am grateful to her for having the courage to share her trials and tribulations, in doing so the black community and particularly the Windrush Generation, know they have a champion who will relentlessly keep turning the dial against racial inequality, mirroring the resilience of that generation whom she has made proud.

Terminology

BBV	Black British Voices
BMA	British Medical Association
BTC	Be That Change
CJS	Criminal Justice System
CPS	Crown Prosecution Service
ECHR	European Commission on Human Rights
EHCR	Equality and Human Rights Commission
ISU	Immigration Service Union
JCHR	Joint Committee on Human Rights
HMRC	His/Her Majesty's Revenue and Customs
LGBT	Lesbian, Gay, Bi-sexual and Transgender
NAO	National Audit Office
NHS	National Health Service
RDR	Race Disparity Report
REN	Race Equality Network
SPC	Safe Space Clinic
SRA	Solicitors Regulatory Authority
WCS	Windrush Compensation Scheme
WJC	Windrush Justice Clinic
WRP	Windrush Reach Project

Prologue

I was fourteen years old, and my teacher asked a question, I eagerly stuck my hand in the air. My white teacher turned to me and said: "Why is your hand up, you don't know the answer." I slowly lowered my hand. It wasn't just the shame and embarrassment that took hold that day, there was an immense frustration, a real sense of disempowered, as I helplessly looked on, and my white classmate confidently provided the same answer that I had prepared.

On my way home, I tried to reason around what happened that day, but the more I thought about it, the angrier I got. Yet the anger I felt was not levelled at my teacher. I was annoyed with myself. Why didn't I say anything? Why did I allow her to dismiss me in such a cold, callous way? Because like most of my black peers, I had accepted the status quo. I was first generation born in Britain, daughter of Jamaican parents, who travelled here in 1962, to begin a new life. My parents, along with thousands of other Caribbeans had high expectations for us, who on the face of it were given the same opportunities as our white counterparts. Benefiting from a British education system that was open to all.

I wanted to make my parents proud, wanted them to believe that I could excel at school, make it to university to study law and fulfil my dream of becoming a lawyer. But this was not a journey I could take alone, because for my ambition to be realised, those responsible for providing me with the tools and skills to reach my goal had to have faith in my ability. I had resigned myself to that never happening because when my teachers saw me, they didn't see a lawyer, they saw a girl, who in their words was "not A-Level material." And by lowering my hand that day, I was somehow complicit in enabling that label to take hold and define me.

I didn't tell my parents what had happened, they had no power, and my teacher held all the cards, could do and say what she wanted. Anyway, who would believe me over her? But the following morning as I walked into class and stood by the window waiting for her to come in, I was filled with resentment. When she entered and told us all to take our seats, I illustrated my displeasure by deliberately taking longer than usual to make my way to my desk. Before sitting down I adjusted my school blazer and made her wait for me, without looking at her once. Which was my way of fighting back. It was wonderful because technically I had done nothing wrong.

After registration, I left the room, and as I passed the teacher I fired a shot across her bows, with a subtle smile, and her face reddened. My actions that morning were more powerful than any screaming or shouting would have been. I was proud of myself, but nothing is ever that simple.

That evening on arriving home, Dad and Mum were waiting for me.

"Yu teacher called today, she said she is concerned that you have an attitude problem."

My teacher knew exactly what she was doing, they had been around Caribbean parents long enough to know how strict they were, and my parents were no different. I was so scared, but I figured I had nothing to lose, so told them about the incident the day before. My parents listened, and I waited for the hammer to fall. But it didn't.

Dad led me into the front room, where he telephoned my teacher. His words will remain with me forever as he told her: "I tink yu are the one with de problem, yu ave a problem wid my daughter."

As Dad laid down the law to my teacher and fought for me, I felt vindicated that they believed me. But I also realised that ironically, just the way my teacher had no faith in me, I lacked that same faith in my parents. It was a misplaced lack of trust because they more than anyone would have understood what I was going through, as they had been through it themselves and continued to deal with racism that existed within British society.

On replacing the receiver Dad turned to me and said: "Yu do know that they are not going to let yu in, and you are going to have to fight and work twice as hard to succeed." He was open and honest about how hard it would be, and I nodded in all the right places, but deep down I was terrified. How does a 14-year-old fight an establishment made up of systems hell-bent on denying you the same opportunities as your white peers? When I returned to school the next day, my teacher made no mention of the conversation she'd had with Dad, and despite her being more guarded in her treatment of me, nothing changed the fact that she marked my papers, wrote my report cards and played an influential role in my young life.

When it comes to the British education system, my white peers began their journey from the same place. Further down the road we hit a fork, in which my white peers took the road leading to opportunity and privilege, whilst my black peers were led to lack of opportunities, and inequality of treatment, fuelled by racism. A road I was on for over 16 years of my life.

Lefty Lawyer shows how I managed to navigate my way off that road, how I eventually found my voice, a way in Dad's words to "fight for success," despite the various bumps and potholes along the way, to become a lawyer at 41 years old. This book shows how I had to push myself, to not take the safe option, of accepting ground rules that society had put in place for me. Rules which defined me as mediocre, unattractive and unworthy of success when pitched against my white counterparts.

Being a lawyer (a solicitor) is a mammoth responsibility and extremely stressful, no matter what colour you are. In writing this book, I hope to take you through my experiences of the last 20 years and show you how the importance of my ancestral historical past has shaped and impacted my career, along with telling you my views on other societal issues. This has, at times, tested me in ways I did not expect, as I have lived in this skin. It isn't just about courage, it's about how with the support and encouragement of others I found a way to ensure I never lowered my hand again.

"Legal hero Pauline Campbell is on a mission for social justice"
Law Society Gazette

"A strong advocate for the Windrush community, Pauline Campbell has provided advice to over 100 victims"
The Times

"Success against the odds"
Woman's Own

PART I
THE IMPORTANCE OF MY VOICE

CHAPTER 1

The Starting Block

In January 2023, I attended a Holocaust Memorial event, where I met Dr Agnes Kaposi, a Holocaust survivor who shared her amazing, heartbreaking, and uplifting journey of survival, tenacity, and courage. Since the event, we have had several enlightening discussions about various perspectives on life, spanning generations.

One day, during one of our in-depth discussions, I confidently told Agnes that I was proud of being black. Agnes looked at me perplexed, before asking: "Why would you be proud of a characteristic you had no control over? Surely, what you should be proud of is the things you have achieved in your life as a person."

I'd never thought about it like that before, but Agnes's words made perfect sense. I realised I had applied the same principle to becoming a black lawyer. I was proud to have finally qualified and gained access to a prestigious profession, where so few black people were present. But in considering my conversation with Agnes, it became clear that although wearing the title of a black lawyer was wonderful, it was about so much more than that.

In 2012, in delivering the commencement address to Spelman College graduates, American talk show host, television producer, actress, author, and motivational speaker, Oprah Winfrey said: "The real truth is that service and the significance that you bring to your service is that which is lasting ... whatever your occupation, job or talent."[1]

Oprah's words resonated with me because they helped to put Agnes's and my conversation into perspective. Being black and a lawyer isn't who I am, it doesn't define me. The only things that can do that are my actions and how I live my life in the service that I bring, and this is why I decided to write this book.

---

1.   Oprah Winfrey, Commencement Address to Class of 2012, Spelman College, Mississippi, 20 May 2012.

In October 2021, I released my first non-fiction book, *Rice and Peas and Fish and Chips*, which I wrote in homage to my Jamaican parents who travelled here in the early-1960s and thousands like them to make a new life for themselves on British shores. The book aimed to give an insight into my journey of being a first generation born in Britain to Jamaican parents. To show how we navigated our way through the social and political racism that existed around us, and the ripple effect this inequality has had on subsequent generations. Taking the reader through an exploration of how I managed to "reboot" myself, break through the barriers, and become a lawyer after being failed by our education system, in which I was told at the age of 15 that I was not A-Level material.

However, as is the case with romantic movies, which end with the couple riding off into the distance or standing in the aisle as they become partners for life, my book abruptly ended with me entering the legal profession I had always dreamed of joining, which many would argue is the perfect ending. We all want to be happy ever after, and I was no different. I had become a lawyer and finally broken through my glass ceiling. Shouldn't that have been enough?

The answer to that is a resounding "No," because that was just the beginning of my journey. And just as *Rice and Peas and Fish and Chips* had provided me with a better awareness of my childhood history and journey into adulthood within British society, to progress, and in Oprah's words "fulfil the highest, truest expression of myself,"[2] I had to explore how, over the past 20 years, I, as a black female lawyer, have plotted my way through a profession in which I have been marginalised, in a profession reluctant to open its doors to more diversity.

In April 2017, JUSTICE produced a report entitled Increasing Judicial Diversity.[3] This was the third report on the judiciary that organization had published in 60 years, with previous reports having been published in 1972[4]

---

2. Ibid.
3. "Increasing Judicial Diversity. A Report by JUSTICE" (2017), chair of the working party, Nathalie Lieven QC.
4. "The Judiciary" (Report of a JUSTICE Sub-Committee) (1972). Which recommended that solicitors and academics should be eligible to take up judicial posts; newly appointed judges should have special training before they first sit; and a consultative committee be formed to assist the Lord Chancellor with judicial appointments.

and 1992.[5] In 1992, Lord Taylor, Lord Chief Justice of England and Wales, said:

> "The present imbalance between male and female, white and black judiciary is obvious…I do not doubt that the balance will be redressed in the next few years…Within five years, I expect to see a substantial number of appointments from both these groups."[6]

More than 30 years on, there has been very little progress. In 2023, the proportion of black judges in the courts and tribunals in England and Wales remained at 1% while the proportion of Asian judges doubled in the same period from 3% to 6%.[7] Other statistics have revealed that individuals of black or black British ethnicity constituted 3% of barristers, 3% of solicitors, and 3% of chartered legal executives.[8] Despite these worrying figures, it's essential to acknowledge the fact that I and others have managed to break through.

But in writing this book, I had to face an uncomfortable truth, one where I had to accept that *I nearly did not make it*. Not just because of the inequality existing within the legal world but because of my self-doubt. A lack of belief that I had a legitimate right to success due to the ripple effects of the ongoing racism and prejudices I had experienced, stemming back to my childhood, which continued to manifest into adulthood.

5. Lord Chief Justice Taylor's Dimbleby Lecture (1992) which publicly acknowledged that the judiciary is unrepresentative, but stated that gender and ethnicity imbalance will be redressed "in the next few years"; "The Judiciary in England and Wales" (Report of the JUSTICE Committee) chaired by Professor Robert Stevens recommended positive action and a commission for judicial appointments to increase diversity.
6. Lord Taylor, "The Judiciary in the Nineties," Richard Dimbleby Lecture (1992), cited by the House of Lords' Select Committee on the Constitution, Judicial Appointments, 25th Report of Session 2010–12.
7. Diversity of the Judiciary: Legal Professions, New Appointments, and Current Post Holders, (2022), Statistics. Updated 13 July 2023. https://www.gov.uk/government/statistics/diversity-of-the-judiciary-2022-statistics/diversity-of-the-judiciary-legal-professions-new-appointments-and-current-post-holders-2022-statistics#overview-of-the-legal-professions-and-judiciary (accessed 2 January 2024). Hilborne, Nick (2023), "Proportion of Black Judges Remains at 1%," *Legal Futures*, July 14. https://www.legalfutures.co.uk/latest-news/proportion-of-black-judges-remains-at-1#:~:text=The%20proportion%20of%20Black%20judges,Ministry%20of%20Justice%20(MoJ) (accessed 2 January 2024).
8. "Diversity of the Judiciary: Legal Professions, New Appointments, and Current Post holders (2022), Statistics. Updated 13 July 2023. https://www.gov.uk/government/statistics/diversity-of-the-judiciary-2022-statistics/diversity-of-the-judiciary-legal-professions-new-appointments-and-current-post-holders-2022-statistics#overview-of-the-legal-professions-and-judiciary (accessed 2 January 2024).

I couldn't shake the feeling that I wasn't good enough. It's hard to admit that my journey as a lawyer began from a place of fear, and looking back it's quite possible that my fellow white graduates would have also been filled with trepidation about what lay ahead. The prospect of entering a world where you would be relied upon as a legal expert, have to attend court, and face judges was a daunting prospect. Like my fellow white graduates, I was heading down a road I had never been on before, and I knew it would be hard enough without me creating my own barriers of inadequacy. Was I justified in feeling this way? Weren't we all starting from the same place as we embarked on a new life, a new career?

The answer to that is "No." Although we had all gone through rigorous exams and professional skills courses, we did not all start from the same place. Unlike my white counterparts, despite years of trying to address the imbalance, I was entering a profession in which the number of people who looked like me was limited. How would I deal with the preconceived ideas of a predominately white profession? A profession where they saw someone who looked like me more often on the accused's side? It was an additional hurdle that I and other black lawyers would have to overcome.

In April 2022, the Commercial Bar Association, Chancery Bar and the Technology and Construction Bar Association published a report, "Specialist Commercial Bar and Black Inclusion, First Steps." Substantive evidence, gathered through questionnaires and roundtables, vividly illustrated the "cultural hurdles and barriers faced by black barristers" characterised by profound levels of isolation, dislocation, and feelings of "not belonging." The evidence also points to high levels of race and ethnicity-related behaviours, including banter, bullying, and discrimination/bias. Surprisingly and disappointingly, high proportions of those who responded to the survey (of all ethnicities) reported direct experience, witnessing, and awareness of such behaviours. A lack of support was also noted, particularly from senior barristers and their clerks/practice managers.[9]

In 2008, Dr Joy DeGruy Leary said:

"We all have our ideas, our beliefs, and then we all have our own experiences. For example, the people of colour in the room are arriving at a

---

9. Jinadu, Abdul-Lateef, Lee Krista QC, Richmond, Jeremy QC, Stevens-Hoare, Brie QC (2022), "The Specialist Commercial Bar and Black Inclusion—First Steps," commissioned by the Royal Bar Association and the Technology and Construction Bar Association, April.

different level because they have lived in this skin. And we rarely receive any level of appreciation and understanding of what you have to live with walking through the world with this skin. So, you come into the room at a different level of awareness."[10]

An awareness that became prevalent within the early stages of my legal career. To qualify, I had to undertake a Legal Practice Course, which I chose to do at the College of Law in Store Street. One day, I had to switch lectures and mistakenly walked into the Commercial Law class. On entering, I immediately knew something was wrong, not just because I was the only black person in the room, but because of the stares from the other students that gave me an uncomfortable feeling that I was unwelcome. Was this my imagination? Was I looking for something that wasn't there? Whatever the reason, I chose not to sit down but walked to the front of the class to check with the lecturer, who politely confirmed that my class was being held in another room, which he directed me to. As I walked towards the door, through that class, followed by the eyes of those young white students, a feeling of disempowerment overwhelmed me. Although I knew it was an honest mistake, and it could have easily been a fellow white student who might have accidentally walked into that room, the question had to be, "Would they have received the same response I did?" Nothing could take away the pain I felt as I closed that door behind me. Whether my conclusions were justified or not, even at that early stage, I could see that when it came to law, there was a clear dividing line between the more lucrative and less lucrative areas of the subject.

A few months later, my thoughts in this regard were further substantiated when I booked an appointment with the College of Law's career service. The career adviser was quite blunt, stating: "There are jobs, voluntary organizations could be useful, and there are always law firms on the high street." Law covers a vast area, but it is also expensive. There are several organizations, such as Law Centres and Citizens Advice offices that provide free legal advice to people in need of legal assistance, covering areas, such as Housing, Immigration, Debt Management. There was also the option of applying to local firms of solicitors on the high street, which might have legal opportunities for someone like me who was newly qualified. But in both cases, income would be extremely low. I also heard horror stories of how

---

10. Dr Joy DeGruy Leary, "Post Traumatic Slave Disorder," Lecture, Terrance Carney. https://www. youtube.com/watch?v=BGjSday7f_8 (accessed 12 January 2022).

some solicitors would take you on as a legal assistant or paralegal, promising a training contract after a year, which never materialised. The careers adviser never bothered to ask me what area of law I was interested in, and she left me with the impression that I should take what I could get. So, I thanked her and left.

But the final blow came just a few months after I had qualified as a solicitor. I decided to try to obtain a role within a larger firm near the City of London. With that in mind, I contacted some of the more prestigious legal recruitment agencies. I had come this far, had been tenacious in working towards my goal, and I believed that the hurdles I had to overcome would make me a credible candidate. I contacted a few agencies and sent in my CV, and when they failed to respond, I called one of them. I spoke to a lady, and after a few moments, she stated: "Maybe you should try another agency; I don't think you are quite what we are looking for."

In November 2022, the Social Mobility Foundation (SMF) reported its findings that law firms are missing out on talent and profit by not taking on graduates from non-professional family backgrounds who attended state schools. Sarah Atkinson, SMF chief executive, said some large law firms still recruit 95% of their graduate intake from elite Russell Group universities.[11]

This established earlier in my legal career how strategically I was manoeuvred away from the more lucrative areas of law in which I wished to practice. None of this was linked to my ability but was purely based on inequitable practices, prejudices, and perceptions linked to my colour and social background.

In 2020, Leslie Thomas, a high-profile black QC (now KC) and first Law Professor at Gresham College, said:

> "If top commercial chambers are predominantly 'white, male and older,' getting a message across to them of change is implicitly saying there is something fundamentally wrong with you. This is a difficult message to swallow. Changing and challenging the status quo is always difficult, particularly from the outside. There has to be a willingness to tackle this from within. But some harsh realities need to be confronted. Firstly, to discuss diversity and improving diversity, particularly as it concerns race, there needs to be a proper and honest discussion about racism…we can pretend if we don't see it, it isn't there. We can be comfortable with the status quo or the cards

---

11. "Law Firms Failing to Improve Social Mobility," *People in Law*, 31 October 2022. https://peopleinlaw.co.uk/law-firms-failing-to-improve-social-mobility/ (accessed 3 January 2024).

we've been dealt. However, the reality is there for all to see if we care to look. We as a profession have to move beyond seeing racism as individual characteristics. We need to understand racism as a system, not an event. None of us are exempt from its forces."[12]

---

12. Rose, Neil, "Your chambers aren't colour blind, top QC tells barristers," *Legal Futures,* 22 June 2020. https://www.legalfutures.co.uk/latest-news/your-chambers-arent-colour-blind-top-qc-tells-barristers (accessed 8 January 2024).

CHAPTER 2

The Resilience to Qualify

After successfully passing my Legal Practice course, the next step was finding work as a trainee solicitor, requiring two years of legal work within a law practice or legal organization. My decision to apply for a training contract outside London was not easy. I wanted to stay in London, but the competition was so stiff that I had to think outside of the box. Adopt the mindset that, hopefully, most people would not be prepared to travel, increasing my chances.

I figured I must have been right when I secured my interview with Kent Magistrates' Courts. This took place in the idyllic surroundings of West Malling, which could not have been more different from the hustle and bustle of Tottenham, where I lived at the time. I prepared hard for the interview, and although my stomach was like jelly, I was confident in answering the questions put to me. To say I was on tenterhooks for the two weeks following the interview would be an understatement. When I finally got the call, I was leaving the dentists and could hardly contain myself when they informed me that I had been successful and was being offered the position.

Working as a legal adviser within the magistrates' courts would give me an in-depth grounding into the legal world because 90% of all criminal cases go through that court. Assault offences, criminal damage, motoring offences, and more serious crimes such as murder, rape, and robbery. All criminal cases start with a first hearing in the magistrates court. Many will stay with the magistrates, while others will be sent to the Crown Court.

Those who decide cases within the magistrates' courts are known as "the bench," which comprises two or three magistrates who are not legally qualified. However, cases are also decided by one legally qualified district judge. The court staff consist of court ushers, who sort out who is in court and make sure cases are ready. Key players within the magistrates' courts also include lawyers from the Crown Prosecution Service (CPS), defence lawyers, probation offic-ers, defendants (the accused), and witnesses. As the legal adviser, I would be required to sit in front of the magistrates, provide legal advice, help ensure the court ran smoothly, and liaise with those in court. I would have to read the charge and ask the defendant to enter a plea. In taking on the role, I had to undertake three months of training, involving sitting with experienced legal advisers for eight weeks before being supervised and assessed for another four weeks. After that I would cover court on my own. I didn't sleep for a week before my first solo run, a traffic court, and was thankful when it was over. But the magistrates and usher were supportive and helped me through, and as the weeks wore on my confidence grew.

However, looking back, I cannot help thinking that I was a little naïve when I applied to Kent. I had never visited that county before obtaining the train-ing contract and knew nothing about the area. But I had applied for so many training contracts that I was terrified I would never obtain a post, conscious that hundreds of applicants would be applying for limited positions.

I had lived and worked in London all my life and didn't consider how dif-ficult it would be to adapt to working within the environment of magistrates' courts, where I would be required to travel between Maidstone, Sevenoaks, and Sittingbourne. In addition, I also had to acclimatise myself to a completely new cultural environment, in which I was one of only two black legal advisers within the courts. The world I grew up in was so diverse, whereas Kent was the complete opposite because I rarely saw anyone who looked like me while working there. However, today is very different, with census figures in 2022 revealing Kent as the seventh most ethnically diverse county in the nation.[1]

There was also an expectation that because I was in my late thirties when I secured the contract, I was better equipped to deal with the change. But that was a misconception because, if anything, it was harder, as I was settled in my ways and was used to a certain standard of living. Before qualifying as a law-yer, I had been a senior housing benefits officer, working on an agency basis on good pay, and the training contract halved my wages. This reduction in income, alongside having to pay back a student loan and increased travelling expenses back and forth to Kent, took a toll on me financially, which is something I

---

1. Hunter, Steve, "Kent ranks 7th as most ethnically diverse city in the nation," *Kent Reporter,* 16 September 2022.

should have factored in before deciding to work outside London. But although concerning, I knew that if I could hold on for the 18 months it would take me to complete the contract, I could return to London. Thankfully, I had a small mortgage at the time and was able to pay most of my bills via direct debit, with holidays off the agenda and all expenditure cut back.

What I also had to face was the social impact this had on me; none of my friends were lawyers, and they all worked in London. During those 18 months, I lost touch with most of them and due to the travelling did not see my family as much.

A huge impact was not working with anyone who looked like me or shared my cultural background, making it extremely hard to be authentic in the environment. My legal colleagues were great, polite, and friendly, but there was a detachment, a gap between us that I could not fill. I was also very conscious that I was a black woman with a strong cockney accent, which, for weeks, I did my best to conceal. But after a while, it became so exhausting that I decided I just needed to be me, and although I let go of trying so hard to conceal the real me, I was still very aware of my blackness in and outside the courtroom. My true personality, the gregarious, confident, and forthright Pauline, was shelved and replaced by a more conservative, toned-down version to help me fit in. However, as my training contract came to an end and I approached the finishing line, I gained a newfound strength in wanting to be the best lawyer I possibly could.

The difficulty I faced was I had no idea where my career would take me. My natural feeling for social justice had never left me, and I knew that whatever role I ended up in I would find a way to use my voice in this area. But I was beginning my legal journey, so I would need to build resilience, develop new traits, and stay true to my values and moral compass. This is a journey we all have to take when we reach that juncture in our lives where we have to decide what kind of person we will be within our professional career, which is not limited to the law. Would I be able to maintain an integral part of my authentic self, or would I have to sacrifice the real me along the way?

In October 2023, the *Voice* newspaper joined forces with Cambridge University and the i-Cubed consultancy. It published a groundbreaking report, "Black British Voices" (BBV), for which 10,000 black people were interviewed to reflect the condition of the black British community today. It revealed that

98% of 8,558 black Brits felt compelled to tone down their black identity to avoid negativity from co-workers and bosses.[2]

Dr Patrick Roach, the general secretary of the teachers' union NASUWT and former chair of the TUC's Anti Racism Taskforce said it was no surprise that black workers had to leave their culture at home despite evidence that diversity is good for business. Stating that black workers having to leave their identity at home was "having a profound impact on the physical and mental well-being of black workers and can have a catastrophic impact."[3]

Sandra Kerr CBE, Race Director at Business in the Community, said: "Having to compromise identity at work is exhausting ... It's the weathering effect; it does wear you down constantly, not being able to be yourself."[4]

Cynthia Davis CBE is the CEO and founder of Diversifying Group, a diversity and inclusion organization, and co-founder of Diversifying Jobs, a job board for social change. She highlighted how, within the BBV report, multiple participants cited an assumption that black employees "cannot deal with responsibility" or "lack leadership skills," stating, "I see time and time again the misconception from employers that to hire employees from a minority ethnic background means lowering the standard of candidates."[5]

In 1981, the Rampton Report,[6] considered the underachievement of Caribbean children within the British educational system, establishing that racism had a direct and vital bearing on the performance of West Indian children, which included teachers' low expectations of these children. The press reactions were critical, with one educational correspondent stating: "They should not have assumed so easily that low achievement of West Indian pupils equal underachievement, as they had gathered no firm statistical data to prove that West Indians are performing at a level below their capabilities."[7]

I was 15 when the Rampton Report began, and I was one of those children who my white teacher told was "not A-Level material." And for years, I bought into that lie. It was a lie that would persist and follow me into adulthood, even after I no longer believed it.

---

2. Black British Voices: i-Cubed, *The Voice*, University of Cambridge, October 2023.
3. Ibid.
4. Ibid.
5. Ibid.
6. "West Indian Children in Our Schools: Interim Report of the Committee of Inquiry into the Education of Children From Ethnic Minority Groups," (The Rampton Report), 1981.
7. Ibid.

Securing the job in Kent as a trainee solicitor was a huge step for me mentally because it took years to find my voice after leaving school with virtually no qualifications. To do that 180 degree switch required a u-turn in my mindset, which I describe as my re-boot in self-belief. But in obtaining the training contract, I had failed to take into account the fact that no matter how far I had come in believing in myself on the road to becoming a lawyer, like my teachers before them, the mindset of some of my white managers remained entrenched in a place in which, when they saw me, they saw someone who lacked ability and a lowering of standards within the profession.

These misconceptions, referred to by Cynthia Davis, played themselves out in many ways while I worked in Kent. On one particular occasion, I was covering court on a three-day trial, which did not go ahead due to the failure of one of the parties. Court time is precious, and as the legal adviser I made the decision that it would be appropriate to prepare what is known as a wasted costs application against that party to cover the time and costs lost by the court. I researched the legal rules and prepared the paperwork, which I presented to a manager. She looked at it and stated without any reason, "This is not a wasted cost." I provided my reasons as to why I felt this was an appropriate way forward. But my manager remained steadfast. On the one hand I had to accept that they were experienced and as such could be right. I was also mindful that maybe paranoia was kicking in on my part, and I should be open to constructive criticism, which I could learn from. But I couldn't ignore the dismissive manner in which I was being treated, which could have been down to the fact that she may just have had a stressful day. The last thing she needed to do was to work her way through a comprehensive wasted costs application. But whatever her reasons, the impact on me was feeling devalued and morally deflated. Was her treatment of me based on the pressures of work, or on me being black? Which is the biggest conundrum, because as a black person, it's impossible not to be affected by racist encounters of the past. It is not always easy to detach yourself from suspicion of others that can be a direct result of that past experience? But although racism may not have factored into how I was treated by my manager that day, the hardest part of being black within the environment in which we work and live is that, because of the subtle way in which racism manifests itself, we will never know, or be in a position to prove it. Even if we believe it played a part in how we have been treated and the detrimental effect it had on how we felt.

Thankfully, for a case of this nature, the decision needed to be made by the head of my service, who read the papers and determined that it was, in fact, a wasted costs situation. Although I was pleased that I had been exonerated, it did not change how deflated I felt by my legal ability being questioned. But what that incident with my manager showed me was I must be on the side of caution when considering whether racism could be applied to how I was being treated. I also had to be acutely aware that it exists within the workplace.

I had been in the job for just over six months, and was asked a question in open court. I wasn't sure of the answer and as such excused myself to check with my manager. On explaining the position, they did not answer, but instead made me follow them into open court, where they stated: "Why are you asking this person the question, they don't know the answer." And then proceeded to answer the question themselves. This was very different to the previous one-to-one scenario with my other manager, as this was questioning my ability to answer a question in open court, and it was scary how similar it was to my teacher, all those years ago, telling me to put my hand down because I didn't know the answer.

As I stood behind this person, I was consumed with anger, I have never been a violent person, but at that moment I wanted to "knock them out." I felt humiliated and disempowered, as everyone's focus was on her and not me, and the worst part of all was that I was then required to continue running a court in which I had been completely undermined. I had to make a choice that day, because I knew if I had done what I wanted to do, I would have lost everything, and all my hard work up to this point would have evaporated into nothing. People mistake silence for weakness, but as I stood behind my manager, saying nothing, it took all my strength and willpower. The pain of that day has never left me, with the worst part being that I had to pick myself up and continue to work with this person because I could not give them the satisfaction of destroying my dream.

Most of us will reach a point in our lives where we will be engulfed by what I describe as the red mist, in which the actions of others are so awful that instinctively we want to lash out against that person. It helps to relieve the stress and tension and provides some form of satisfaction. But when you get to that point, you need to stop and think. Give yourself the time you need to understand the best way forward. By no means will this be easy, but if your future could be threatened by a rash decision, then "it's just not worth it." Any gratification will be short lived, but your regret will last for a lifetime.

Of course there will be side effects in holding back. For me, the ripple effect was that my confidence was shattered, and I took a downward spiral; I dreaded going to work, taking the hour-and-a-half journey down the M20, M25 and M2. I was terrified of making mistakes because if an error did occur in a court in which I was sitting, I would be admonished for it, irrespective of the fact that I was a trainee and a more experienced colleague had been present and had advised me at the time. With that in mind, if I was running a late court, I would work into the night to make sure all my cases were updated with the court results to ensure I would not be accused of delay. I would read and re-read my files despite the long drive. I would be the first one in every morning. If I was running a court that had cases I was not familiar with, I would come in extra early to meet with the prosecutors to go through them and any legislation I was not sure of, so I was prepared for the day. In order to keep my head above water, I guess I worked twice as hard as everyone else despite living the furthest away.

After gruelling months following this routine, I concluded that my life would be easier if I returned to London. Therefore, I chose to seek a transfer as a trainee solicitor in the role of a legal adviser in the London courts. Granted, there were no guarantees that I would not come across similar issues, but at least in London I would be in a more diverse environment with people who I felt better understood cultural differences. Yet no matter how hard I tried, it was impossible because the competition was just too great. I met with a good friend and confided in them about how I was feeling and how unhappy I was and, being the good friend they were, they encouraged me to hold on and not give up on my dream.

But as the months wore on, although I worked as hard as I could, my health began to suffer as my confidence continued to wane, and the travelling took its toll. My car was giving me problems, so I booked it into the garage at seven in the morning, to make sure I could catch the 8.30 am train to Kent. I was shattered, having worked late the night before, but I could not take the chance of not getting to work on time. I left the house at 6.30 am that morning to get the car to the garage, which thankfully had a key drop-off station. I made it to Kings Cross and got into work in time for the video court, which I had to cover that day.

The video link was all set when I arrived in court. When I switched the camera on, I noticed I looked extremely dark. The usher and I tried to adjust it, but nothing worked. It was awful, and the problem was made worse by the fact that I was wearing a white shirt and black suit, which, along with my teeth, glared out on camera. I felt sick as I could hear the correctional officers and the defendants laughing on the other end of the link. I wanted to dig a hole and hide in it. Frantically trying to adjust the brightness was only making things worse. I felt humiliated and ashamed, not because I was black, but due to the fact that there was nothing I could do to remedy the distorted image. As the court legal adviser I had to keep my camera on the entire time, with the bench directly behind me. I sat through four cases that afternoon, which seemed to last forever. It was frustrating how little thought is placed on black people when systems are put in place and just because no-one of my colouring had worked there before. Black people are an integral part of society, and as such, adjustments should have been in place on my arrival.

As soon as the court had ended, I went straight to the office manager along with my manager and made it clear that I would not appear on another video link until the lighting had been adjusted. They were both extremely apologetic, and the problem was remedied in time for my next sitting. But all I could hear on the train home that night was the laughter and the embarrassed looks of the other people in the courtroom. It took me half an hour to walk to the garage, as for some reason there were no buses. My feet were killing me, as I had forgotten to put my trainers in my bag that morning. I needed to write up my cases, so I stayed at court quite late. Therefore, I didn't get to the garage until after 8 pm, which was now closed. However, as I had paid over the phone, security gave me my keys, and I got back home at 9.30 pm.

On arriving home I collapsed on the sofa in a flood of tears. I decided that night enough was enough, and a year into my contract I handed in my resignation. The reason I gave for this was that the travelling was just too much for me, and was affecting my health, particularly as I was required to drive between Maidstone, Sevenoaks, and Sittingbourne. Taking the long drive home after a busy day in court was proving more and more difficult. On making the decision, I felt relief that I was going to come home. To me, it wasn't a sense of failure. I had already completed a whole year, which would be counted as credit. Although it might take a while, I was confident that I would find a new trainee position in London where I could complete my training.

My notice had been handed in, and I was due to leave in ten weeks; I had been in court that morning and was preparing for the afternoon list when one of my managers came in to speak to me. The manager pulled up a chair and told me they felt that I was making a mistake in handing in my notice, as they encouraged me to stay. They told me it would be awful to stop now when I was so close to qualifying. The truth is, I knew they were right, but they were not privy to the real reason why I had decided to leave. I wanted to tell them about how I felt constantly undermined, about the humiliating incidents I had to face in court, and how they had scared me. They knew about the video link, but as with everything else, I played that down and didn't let them know how deeply it had impacted me. In all honesty, I could not trust them. I thanked the manager for coming to speak to me and promised I would think about it.

My Dad always said that if you have an important decision, you should think with your head and not your heart. That night, as I considered what had been said, I realised that I was being tested, and that at some point in all our lives we get to this point in which a decision we make could have ramifications for the rest of our lives. The key to my decision had to rest with the most important thing I wanted, which took centre stage over everything else. The answer was, "I wanted to become a lawyer." I then considered all the time and money invested into getting to this point in my life. Lastly, I thought about my parents and how they had so many high hopes for me as a child, how until the age of 14 I had excelled academically, and how I had let them down when it all went so wrong. I was determined not to let them down again.

After a few days and much deliberation, I went to work and withdrew my resignation. Was I wrong in failing to confide in my manager all those years ago about my isolation, the lack of belief in me, as well as the humiliation I had experienced at the hands of those who should have provided me with help and support? I believe I was also mistaken in feeling compelled to tone myself down within my working environment.

No. I wasn't wrong because I had no tangible evidence to show that my treatment was linked to racism. The video link was an unintentional technical issue, which, although it showed ignorance of diversity, was an honest mistake that was rectified as soon as it was brought to their attention. But they could never take away the humiliation of it. That was something I just had to live with. Even with the questioning of my abilities and that awful incident, where I was undermined, I had not said anything at the time, so any allegation would likely be met with staunch denial.

A friend recommended a great book called *Feel the Fear and Do it Anyway*[8] written by Susan Jeffers PhD, which really helped me navigate my way through this difficult time. The book said:

> "It is reported that over 90% of what we worry about never happens. That means our negative worries have less than 10 per cent of being correct. If this is so, isn't being more positive more realistic than being more negative. Why be miserable when you can be happy? We create our own reality."[9]

I read the book alongside some amazing affirmations from aspiring mentors such as Maya Angelou and Oprah Winfrey, which helped me to focus on the positive, to pour all my energy into reaching my goal of getting through the months ahead. I also put practical steps into place to support me on my journey. A colleague suggested that to ease the pressure on the travelling, I should use leave to take long weekends every other week, whenever possible, on Monday or Friday, which helped. I also spent more time with my family and friends at weekends, rather than sitting at home stressing out about the week ahead. It was good to be around them, and it made me value the importance of the support mechanisms around me.

This was an important lesson on my journey, because up until that point there was a tendency to take my family and friends for granted. I failed to value the important role they played in my life. I held back, and initially didn't share how I was feeling because I didn't want to appear weak or a failure. But as soon as I began to let go of those insecurities, I could tap into the valuable resource of support they could provide at a time when I needed it.

As a trainee, I was required to keep a weekly note of my training. Initially, I would describe what I had done and my learning experience. I decided to add

---

8. Jeffers, Susan (2007), *Feel the Fear and Do it Anyway*, Vermilion.
9. Ibid: pp. 68–69.

a positive personal statement at the end of every week. This illustrated how my abilities as a legal adviser were being enhanced, which showed my communication skills when dealing with difficult defendants, how I always completed my case notes at the end of each day, despite having to factor in extended travelling time. Each week, I would try to add something positive about how I excelled in my role because this became more about how I saw myself than how others saw me.

Of course, there were still bad days when I had to push harder than others to get through, a comment, a look, something that would hurt and bring uneasiness, but my focus was on becoming a lawyer. And I did it. The day I qualified was the day I left Kent as I will explain later.

In 2017, Baroness Ruby McGregor-Smith said:

> "Overt racism that we associate with the 1970s does still disgracefully occur, but unconscious bias is much more pervasive and potentially more insidious because of the difficulty in identifying it or calling it out."[10]

However, what could be determined as the greatest injustice of the impact of racism within the workplace is the loss of talent in respect of those who, like me, decide to leave. In 2021, a report revealed that mid-ranking black lawyers in the UK's largest law firms were four times as likely to leave than their white peers. This according to research tracking the attrition of ethnic minority legal staff from top-tier groups. Data from 35 of the UK's most prominent law firms, including the elite "Magic Circle" (Allen & Overy, Clifford Chance, Linklaters, and Freshfields), showed a fall in black lawyers years after they qualified. "Attrition for junior black lawyers is significantly higher than for other ethnic minority and white lawyers," said Rare, the diversity recruitment company that analysed the data. It noted "clear spikes in the attrition of black lawyers" at the qualification stage and for third and seventh-year associates. That, in turn, led to a lower proportion of black lawyers at partner level.

"By [seven years post-qualification], very few black lawyers left," Rare said. According to the study, half the black lawyers who qualified in 2016 have since

---

10. "Race in the Workplace: The MacGregor Smith Review" (2017), 28 February. https://www.gov.uk/government/publications/race-in-the-workplace-the-mcgregor-smith-review (accessed 4 January 2024).

left, compared with 12% of white lawyers who qualified in the same year. Rare's data did not reveal where the black lawyers who left their roles ended up but showed they had not moved to another of the firms in the survey.[11]

Losing talent is never suitable for organizations. Would I have stayed in Kent if I had been treated better? It's doubtful because being part of the diversity that London had to offer was extremely important to me, and crucially, I wanted to be near my family. A Government-commissioned report in 2017 by Conservative peer Baroness Ruby McGregor Smith found the British economy was losing £24 billion a year, or 1.3% of Gross Domestic Product, through lost potential due to racism in employment.[12]

It's concerning to think of those who have voluntarily left the profession due to negative experiences, and it is equally concerning to think about how that decision may have impacted their lives, about how they view a profession in which they started with so many aspirations and had fought so hard to enter. But there is also a darker side to how misconceptions of black lawyers can lead to devastating effects, in which employees' abilities and conduct results in a threat and loss of their livelihood.

---

11. Beioley, Kate, "UK law firms lose four times as many black lawyers as other ethnicities, exodus from industry at early years results in less diversity at senior levels," *Financial Times*, 17 November 2021.
12. "Race in the Workplace": see earlier footnote.

CHAPTER 3

The Dangers of Unconscious Bias Within the Legal World

As a legal adviser running a court, you can please some people some-times, but you cannot please all of them all of the time. I and my colleagues would have to deal in open court with differing opinions on legal issues. However, the magistrates will ultimately take the advice of the legal adviser, who sometimes needs to be double-checked. Before entering the legal profession, I imagined it would be very different, and it would be akin to the courtroom dramas you see on TV, with twists and turns at every angle. But the reality was very different, with the plethora of paperwork and endless court lists.

A few months before I was due to qualify, I covered court and advised the magistrates on a case where the Crown prosecutor disagreed with me. We discussed the issues in open court. I had given the same advice previously on several occasions and was aware that my colleagues had also done the same when faced with the legal issue concerned. I explained the position, confirm-ing that we would proceed based on the advice I had given, and the prosecutor was not happy and refused to accept my advice, continuing to argue with me in open court. It was difficult because the magistrates were present then, and it was not professional for us to argue back and forth in front of them.

At that point, when I realised the prosecutor had no intention of backing down, I decided to ask them to leave the courtroom. It was a tough decision, but I was regrettably left with no choice. The prosecutor was understandably upset, but in doing so I explained the position to the magistrates and completed my advice. The prosecutor was then permitted to return to the room, where the decision and how it was reached was explained to him.

I wrote a detailed account of the incident, along with the advice given and how I decided to ask that they leave. Although I was a toned-down version of myself, I knew that it was crucial that I was assertive and strong, which for a black woman could be seen as aggressive or angry. My colleagues were supportive, and my managers never questioned my decision.

A couple of weeks later, I attended the same court and was pulled to one side by a prosecutor, who confided in me that a group of prosecutors had filed a complaint against me with their managers at the CPS relating to my conduct in court. The news came as a shock because I had never had any complaints lodged against me as a legal adviser. I considered it may have something to do with the incident two weeks before but could not be sure. Having any complaint against you is concerning enough but being told a group of prosecutors had made a complaint left me dumbfounded. Although I was upset and hurt, even though this had happened I once again focused on the positive: I kept meticulous notes on all my cases. The advantage was my weekly training diary, which was checked by senior management.

Over the coming weeks, I waited for one of my managers to approach me regarding the complaint, but no-one ever did. I assumed that the allegations had been investigated, and nothing found, which I was confident was the case, but I was perplexed that the complaint was never brought to my attention. Due to confidentiality, I could never divulge that I knew about it, and the prosecutor who spoke to me stated they heard no more about it.

It was challenging walking into court after that. Knowing that any of those prosecutors could have complained about me that, if proven, could have placed my hopes of becoming a fully qualified lawyer at risk. I knew that any complaint would have been unfounded because I had done nothing wrong and had acted openly, and the decisions were made in open court. Still, the fact that someone decided to complain, bearing in mind the consequences it could have had on me, was hard to reconcile. I was just at the beginning of my career, and to have any stain on my work as a trainee solicitor could have affected my prospects.

In June 2023, the Solicitors Regulatory Authority (SRA) published an independent review that investigated why there was an overrepresentation of black, Asian, and minority ethnic solicitors concerning complaints (and potential misconduct) to the SRA within their enforcement process. The report revealed a limited evidence base relating to the causes of overrepresentation of minority ethnic groups in complaints about misconduct made to regulators, despite the widespread recognition of patterns of overrepresentation across multiple professions.

One potential explanation for this was socio-cognitive biases, which relate to how a person's cultural or social background may influence their conscious and unconscious perceptions or expectations of others. Some examples of common biases are that women are weak (despite many being very strong). Another is that black people are dishonest (when most are not), are more prone to violent acts, and lack intellectual ability. It is concerning how deep these perceptions go and how damaging they can be, but it is also worrying how they could be argued to be entrenched within our history.

An article written by Robin Whitburn and Abdul Mohamud on Britain's involvement with New World slavery and the transatlantic slave trade noted that as soon as the Europeans began to exploit Africans as enslaved people, racist ideas emerged to justify what they were doing.[1] In 1768, outspoken Anglican Reverend William Knox stated:

"Whether the creator originally formed these black people a little lower than other men, or that they lost their intellectual powers through disuse, I will not assume the province of determining, but certain it is, that a new negro (as those lately imported from Africa are called) is a complete definition of indolent stupidity."[2]

In her lecture, Post Traumatic Slave Disorder, Dr Joy DeGruy Leary took us to the work of Homo Von Linnaeus (1707–1778), a Swedish scientist who developed a system of criteria based on skin colour which laid the basis for 19th century racial classification. Linnaeus determined that there were four families of man, each with peculiarities.

The Homo American Indian was described as reddish, obstinate, contented, and regulated by custom; Homo Europeans were white, fickle, confident, blue-eyed, gentle, and governed by law; Homo Asians were shallow, grave, dignified,

---

1. Mohamud, Abdul and Whitburn, Robin (2018), "Britain's Involvement with New World Slavery and the Transatlantic Slave Trade," *Themes Travel, Colonialism and Slavery, Politics, and Religion,* 21 June.
2. Knox, William, Vassar Rena, "William Knox's Defense of Slavery (1768)," Vol. 114 No. 4, 20 August 1970, pp. 310–326, American Philosophical Society.

greedy, and ruled by opinion; and Homo Africans were black, cunning, lazy, lustful, careless, and governed by impulse.

Dr Leary stated to those who needed to legitimise the act of slavery that Linnaeus's theory provided the proof for, wanted to establish that, scientifically, they were justified in treating slaves as chattel.[3] Further alleged scientific theories around black inferiority came in the guise of Johann Fredrich Blumenbach (1752–1840), a scientist who cited colour, hair, skull, and facial characteristics as a fundamental means of classifying the five varieties of man. His research in the measurement of skulls led him to divide mankind into five great families: Caucasian, Mongolian, Malayan, Ethiopian, and American. Central to Blumenbach's study was the Caucasian, the white European, a term which he originated. He took the name Caucasian from Mount Caucasus because its southern slope had cradled what he felt was the most beautiful race of men, the Georgians. The Caucasus near Mount Ararat, upon which the biblical Ark of Noah came to rest after the flood, seemed the appropriate source for the original race of man, founded on the premise of white superiority. Neither of the theories put forward by Linnaeus nor Blumenbach were based on scientific facts. Still, it's frightening how the myth of black people's tendency to violence and lack of intellect has continued to persist through so-called science.

In 2018, an article written for the *Guardian* by Gavin Edwards discussed the re-emergence of the theory of "race science" or, in many cases, "scientific racism": a theory that argues that black people fare worse than white people because they tend to be less naturally intelligent. Edwards states that these ideas are championed mainly by those at the right-wing end of politics. What's interesting about this theory is if it is believed that poor people are poor because they are inherently less intelligent, then it is easy to leap to the conclusion that liberal remedies, such as positive action or foreign aid, are doomed to fail.

In 2020, the Social Metrics Commission found that nearly half (46%, 900,000 people) of all people living in families where the household head was black/African/Caribbean/black British were in poverty, compared to just under one in five (19%) of those living in families where the head of household was white. In 2022, an analysis by the Runnymede Trust found that people from ethic minority backgrounds are 2.5 times more likely to be in relative poverty

---

3. Dr Joy DeGruy Leary, "Post Traumatic Slave Disorder," Lecture, Terrance Carney. https://www. youtube.com/watch?v=BGjSday7f_8 (accessed 12 January 2022).

(individuals who have income below 60% of the median) and 2.2 times more likely to live in deep poverty (an income more than 50% below the relative poverty line).[4] My first instinct was to treat theories such as scientific racism with the contempt they deserved, but I had no choice but to address the elephant in the room. For centuries, black people have been disproportionately impacted by ongoing poverty, which has taken hold within the black community. Could this be down to a lack of intellectual prowess on our part? Are we using racism as an excuse to hide our inadequacies, which have kept us trapped in poverty?

The answer to that is a definite "No." I was assessed as educationally inadequate and not bright enough to attend university. The biggest mistake I made was believing that assessment for nearly two decades. It was a period in my life where I doubted my capabilities. This didn't just affect my earning capacity; it also took away my belief that I had a right to deserve more. And it was only when I wanted to "change lanes" and take a new career path in the legal profession, which would not only increase my earning capacity but also give me more credibility within the work environment, that I realised how dangerous theories such as scientific racism, which began for me at the age of 15, had continued to take hold. It's scary how deep that goes.

Edward points to an article written in July 2016 by Steve Bannon, who would go on to become US President Donald Trump's chief strategist, during Trump's first term in office, in which Bannon suggested that some black people who the police had shot might have deserved it. "There are, after all, in this world, some people who are naturally aggressive and violent," Bannon wrote, evoking one of scientific racism's ugliest contentions: that black people are more genetically predisposed to violence than others.[5] I, like most people, have seen newspapers filled with the alarming levels of urban knife crime in the UK committed by young black youth. But does that give credence to the fact that black people are more likely to commit violent acts than their white

---

4. BME Statistics on Poverty and Deprivation (2024), Institute of Race Relations, last updated 25 April 2024.

5. Edwards, Gavin (2018), "The unwelcome revival of 'race science'", *Guardian* long read, 2 March. https://www.theguardian.com/news/2018/mar/02/the-unwelcome-revival-of-race-science (accessed 11 January 2022).

counterparts? In her article "Gangs and Knife-Crime Fear: How Has Britain Responded Through History?"[6] Dr Judy Rowbotham stated:

> "Looking back at the past century, you will find that moral panics over crime levels are far from uncommon. They occur when a particular type of crime is suddenly perceived as unusually threatening, often due to the rise of a new technology or tactic. So, while moped crime generated a blizzard of headlines last summer, in the more distant past, bicycles were at the centre of a crime panic, just as railways were when they spread across Victorian Britain. New crime strategies are fodder for the sensational reportage that sells newspapers."[7]

My experiences within Kent reinforced these misconceptions, which in one incident was directly aimed at me. It was a Friday morning and, the night before, the Swedish store Ikea had opened their biggest store in Europe at midnight in Edmonton, with hundreds of cut-price items up for grabs. The fireworks went off as six thousand shoppers, black people and white people, waited anxiously for the doors to open. But it all ended in disaster, as the doors opened, the crowds went mad, people were injured, nine ambulances were called, and the shop, which was scheduled to be opened for 24 hours, had to be closed within 30 minutes. I was unaware of the opening; I was fast asleep, knowing I had to drive to Kent while running court the following morning.

I heard what had happened on the morning news and, on entering court, the comments from barristers and lawyers came thick and fast. They'd listened to what had happened in my neck of the woods, and how did I fare? Did I manage to grab a TV or something along those lines? Of course, as the only black person in court and I was also from Tottenham at the time, I was considered fair game for the butt of their jokes. As my blood began to boil, the authentic me would have happily told them a few home truths in a language they would never forget, but of course, I had to ensure I maintained professionalism. As the insults continued, I suddenly said: "For your information, black and white people were in that queue. You haven't got a clue what you are

---

6. Rowbotham, Judith (2018), "Gangs and Knife Crime Fears: How Britain Responded Through History?," September, *BBC History Magazine*, published online 7 October 2019, BBC, History Extra.
7. Ibid.

talking about. My Dad has more common sense in his little finger than all of you put together." It had the desired effect because they looked embarrassed and said nothing about it.

For me, Dad was the polar opposite of the negative perceptions held about black people; he was a strong, honest, hardworking man. He was one of the brightest men I knew; he could add things up in his head faster than I ever could. He worked hard as a plasterer, became self-employed, and made a good living for his family. He would drive all over London to complete plastering jobs, and sometimes, on a Sunday, he would pack us up in the family car and drive out to the country to show us where he would be working over the coming months. There was no map Dad could not read; back then, it was A to Zs. No SatNavs or Googlemaps existed. Before coming to England, he ran an orchard and food business in Jamaica, where he grew goods and employed workers, supplying local hotels. But coming to England changed all that; there were no opportunities for someone like him to become a businessman in the 1960s when he arrived.[8] The only work available for Dad and those like him was unskilled labour, so when he got a job on a building site, he watched the plasterers and learned the trade with the help of an Irish plasterer. Thinking back to those lawyer's derogatory comments that day, who had all the advantages Dad never had, still hurts. Just because they had managed to carve out a legal career, did that mean they were more intelligent than Dad? No. It did not. It simply meant they were given opportunities people from my parent's generation never had.

Although I have not been furnished with the evidence of why complaints against solicitors are made, it is by no means a stretch of the imagination to conclude that the overrepresentation of black, Asian, and minority ethnic solicitors within the SRA enforcement processes is somehow linked to common bias held by historical and modern beliefs. That somehow black lawyers are less capable than their white counterparts and more prone to make mistakes or be dishonest, so that ultimately could lead to complaints being made based on those misconceptions.

But it's shocking to see how prejudicial racist views against solicitors can manifest. In September 2020, Cavan Medlock allegedly visited the offices of

---

8.   For more on this see, Campbell, Pauline (2021), *Rice and Peas Fish and Chips*, Twenty-Seven.

Duncan Lewis Solicitors in Harrow, armed with a single knife, and threatened to kill a member of staff. The prosecution alleged Medlock planned to take a solicitor hostage and display flags of Nazi Germany and the US Confederacy in the firm's windows to inspire others to carry out similar offences. Medlock allegedly blamed lawyers at the firm for preventing the removal of immigrants from the UK. Days earlier, the then Home Secretary, Priti Patel, had claimed activist lawyers were frustrating the removal of refused asylum seekers from the UK. [9]

Unconscious bias in any form is of concern in every respect. When it runs alongside racism it makes for a dangerous cocktail, which leads to devastating effects for not just black lawyers but all lawyers representing their clients.

---

9. Taylor, Diane (2020), "Man faces terror charge over alleged attack at immigration law firm," *Guardian*, 23 October.

CHAPTER 4

Face-to-Face with My First Black Defendant

A few years before I qualified as a solicitor, I was struck down with an awful stomach bug that took hold of me for three weeks. It got so bad that, at one point, my parents had to take me to hospital. During that time, I lost a lot of weight. Thankfully, I got better, and before returning to work I went to see my doctor for the final okay. I liked my doctor; he was pretty young and was always welcoming. I was worried about my lost weight and asked his advice on what I should do.

"Oh, you'll be fine," he said. "You just need to watch your diet and eat healthy. Also, it would be good to exercise. Swimming's good. Oh, but black people don't swim because they are heavy-boned."

When my doctor said those words, it was in such a matter-of-fact way that I believed that in saying what he did he had no idea he was being racists. Rightly or wrongly, in his mind, he was stating what he thought was a medical fact. This has been based on the premise that people of African descent have thicker, denser bones, which impedes their buoyancy: "Black bones are less likely to break and more likely to sink."[1]

Clearly, at the time, my doctor had no historical knowledge of a man named Jacques Francis, an African diver who dispelled the myth that black people can't swim. In 1546, as part of a group of African salvage divers, he plunged to the depths in the Solent to retrieve Henry VIII's valuable guns from the doomed Mary Rose.[2] But notwithstanding Francis's achievements, my doctor's comments on that day illustrated the subtlety of racism in its most acute form. Showing how it can creep up on you when you least expect it. The most challenging aspect was that I did not know how to respond, so I made the conscious

---

1.   Shultz, Jaime (2019), "Racialized Osteology and Athletic Aptitude, or 'Black' Bones as Red Herrings," *Journal of Sport History*, Vol. 46, No. 3 (Fall), pp. 325–346.
2.   Kaufman, Miranda (2017), *Black Tudors*, Oneworld Publications.

decision to say nothing, which I had to accept was a serious failure on my part. I learned about Jacques Francis, and I knew my doctor was talking twaddle, but the truth was I did not want to confront it. This was *my* doctor, and I did not want to fall out with him or make my life difficult. Looking back, I realise I took the coward's way out, with the pity being he may have had more respect for me had I told him how I felt. Importantly, I could have educated him in a way only a black person could.

Maybe if another black person had been in the room, it would have changed the dynamics, not only giving me courage but also providing me with the support of another person with the same lived experience—someone who would have understood exactly how I felt at the time.

It was a Monday afternoon, and I was just a few months into my training contract in Kent. On the day in question, I worked at Maidstone, in Court One, the central court. It was a splendid courtroom for the three magistrates, with mahogany walls and three magnificent chairs that took centre stage on top of a platform. I sat just below them in an oversized chair overlooked by the court crest, *Dieu et Mon Droit*, which means "God and My Right." Although I had looked at it many times, I never really considered the true meaning of it. Like everything linked to the legal world within the UK, it was part of a tradition that went back hundreds of years. Now I was a part of that institution and all that it encompassed.

The CPS and defence solicitors confirmed they were ready, and I signalled to the usher that I was prepared for the next case to be called. It had been a long day with a number of cases listed, and I prayed we would finish the day in time for me to hit the motorway as early as possible. I pulled out the paper file containing the name of the defendant, who was in custody and, therefore, was being brought into court from the cells. I prepared my papers, entering my name and address, in readiness for their arrival. It was a far cry from the current modern process of tapping a name or number into a computer, where all the information you require suddenly appears before you. I heard the keys jingle in the lock of the dock, but my head was down as I read that pleas were to be entered and a bail application was also to be made.

I looked up. Behind the glass window, with two security guards on either side of him, was a tall, dark, well-built black man. Sometimes, life throws you a curve ball, hitting you with something you don't expect. Until that moment,

I had lived in a bubble, one consumed with a naïvety that had mistakenly propelled me into a world that did not depict the society in which I had lived all my life. Working in Kent had given me a false impression of the make-up of those caught up within the Criminal Justice System (CJS) because, unbelievably, this was the first time in all my months as a trainee that I had come face-to-face with someone who looked like me.

It was a feeling that could only be described as an awakening for me as we stared at each other, with him on one side of the dock and me on the other. I had to collect my thoughts because, despite the differences between our status within Courtroom One, it was impossible to ignore the inextricable link that existed between us, an affinity that I saw behind his eyes and what he must have seen in mine, knowing we were the only two black people present.

I asked him his name and address and then read the charges against him to the court, and he entered a plea of not guilty. I advised him to sit down, and the prosecutor ran through the facts of the case and gave reasons why they opposed the bail application. His defence barrister then stood to their feet, valiantly defending this man's right to be given his freedom until the trial date. Throughout this process, I made copious notes to ensure I could advise the magistrates on any questions they may have. I did everything I was required to do, and as with any case, I did it to the best of my ability.

After consideration, the magistrates refused the bail application, and he was remanded in custody. As the chair of the bench relayed their decision to him, the expression on his face was calm before being taken back down to the cells, where he would then be transported to prison. I watched as the two guards led him away and again heard the jangling keys as they locked the dock behind them. I completed the relevant bail forms and, as if on automatic pilot, the court list.

The end of the day required that I go through the day with the magistrates to ensure they were happy with how the list was run; it also allowed them to ask me any questions. I entered their room and sat with the three of them, made up of one man and two women. We ran through the list; as expected, they were professional and polite. I ran through the list and said something along the lines of: "Nothing unusual that needs highlighting in today's list your worships."

They all agreed, and I thanked them for sitting and left. But as I walked back to my office, packed my case, and put on my coat. I knew I had lied because the day had been highly unusual, leaving me confused. I played my music all the way home and focused on the tunes to keep my mind off how I felt.

That night, I lay awake in bed, trying to fathom what had happened to me. I was terrified at how I was feeling, and it was only in the pitch-black stillness of the night that I finally accepted what I felt: guilt. Guilt that contained a double-edged sword, in which on one side lay the Pauline who believed in the law and everything it stood for and was prepared to work as hard as she could to practice and join the Roll of Solicitors, the coveted record where all solicitors regulated by the SRA is kept, but on the other, there was the Pauline, who had experienced and lived with racism all her life, who had watched her brothers and their friends stopped and searched, be handcuffed and arrested just for talking back. Who, now, was experiencing that racism within the legal world in which I worked, leaving me isolated and alone—a person who knew what it meant to be undermined and have their ability questioned.

That day, I was faced with my worst fear: someone who looked like me, a black face and all that entailed, but they were on one side of the fence and I was on the other. Yet we were the only two black people in court, which made us both vulnerable, even be it for different reasons.

I got up, went downstairs, and made a cup of tea. It was twelve o'clock, and I knew I had work the following morning, but my restlessness made it impossible to settle. I sat on the living-room sofa, determined to reason my way through this mammoth problem. Growing up in Tottenham and now working within the court system, I of all people should have had an understanding and empathy for any black person caught up in the CJS. I realised I had to be extremely cautious in how this empathy manifested itself, about how I did my job because as the Code of Conduct for Solicitors requires: "You do not unfairly discriminate by allowing your personal views to affect your professional relationships and how you provide your services."[3]

The starting point had to be from the perspective of the law. I had no idea whether this man was innocent or guilty. Still, I did know that everyone, no matter what colour, has a right to equal treatment under the law, and as a legal adviser within the magistrates' courts it was my duty to dispense that.

---

3. Rule 1 SRA Code of Conduct for Solicitors. Solicitors Regulation Authority. https://www.sra. org.uk/solicitors/standards-regulations/code-conduct-solicitors/ (accessed 5 January 2024).

But I had to consider my connection to this black defendant equally, and any others I may encounter in the future. It was likely that they, like me, would have also, at some point in their lives, experienced some form of racism, which, unless you experience it, you can never understand. Was I capable of detaching myself from that? Facing this aspect of my future as a lawyer was a massive learning curve for me. Granted, when faced with my first black defendant, I did my job and treated him the same as I would any defendant, but my feelings of guilt and empathy could not simply be ignored.

In 2006, the BBC aired a documentary entitled "Battle for Brixton" about the 1981 Brixton riots. This provided a candid account of what led to the riots in April 1981 through eyewitness testimony from the community and the police. "I didn't join the police to be a racist," said a constable from Brixton at the time, "But while I was in the police, I became one … People had no chance of proving their innocence; evidence was planted, that was a common practice, and assaulting people was almost a daily occurrence."[4] One sergeant who was there in 1981 said: "We were the occupying army if you like and thinking of the people of Brixton as the enemy. That there wasn't a good person amongst them. That they were all criminals … blackness equated with criminality."[5]

I had grown up in Tottenham and had looked on helplessly as police searched my brothers on their way home from school. Just as the police saw black people as the enemy, as a child and growing into adulthood, I looked at them in the same way. How can we not be influenced by the environment around us, and would I allow my negative experiences of the police and my lack of trust for those in Kent to prevent me from doing my job with complete neutrality?

A few weeks later, I got my answer. I was covering court when I received a call that a 15-year-old youth had been remanded in custody. Youth courts have special rules attached to them, and a magistrate sitting had to be specifically trained to deal with youth cases. I dealt with the adult list on this particular day, but my magistrates were also instructed to cover the youth court. I was told that I would need to deal with it, as the young girl was being transferred to a centre run by the local authority but needed to be placed before the magistrates ahead of this being done. I had not dealt with the youth before, but to ensure she was remanded, I needed to provide the necessary paperwork was

---

4. "Battle for Brixton, Brixton Riots" Documentary (2006), BBC2, producer Ed Jarvis.
5. Ibid.

completed once the magistrates had granted the required order. This courtroom did not have a dock, so when the girl was brought in, she was made to sit in the court with security. Before she entered the room, I could hear her shouting, and when she entered, there before me was a young black girl yelling at security to leave her alone. The usher approached me and whispered: "She's trouble." And told me to be careful. The chair of the magistrates asked her to calm down, and she did for a while but then became irate as the prosecutor began to provide the court with details of the charges against her.

The only two black people in the courtroom were myself and the young black girl; everyone else was white, and I knew that I had to find a way to calm her down. At that point, I asked the magistrates if they wouldn't mind retiring for a moment, which they agreed to do, and when they were out of the room I made my way over to the young girl, with security still on either side of her. This is not something that a legal adviser would be required to do, but for me, the wellbeing of this young girl had to be considered. I introduced myself to her and told her it was important that she understand that I was the legal adviser, and she had to believe me when I told her that I knew how she was feeling. Security allowed me to sit next to her, at which point I told her that she must calm down and remember that, in life, she had a choice and could be whatever she wanted. She looked at me and didn't say anything for a while but then said: "Alright, but just tell them not to manhandle me." I got up and told her again, "Remember, in life, we make our own choices. It's hard, but you can be whatever you want if you put your mind to it."

In all my years as a lawyer, I believe those words to be one of the most important things I have ever said to anyone. For the hearing, the girl was calm and polite, and when she left, I gave her a nod to let her know I was proud of her. I have no idea what happened to her, but at the end of the court, the magistrates and court staff congratulated me on calming her down. But I didn't need any words of thanks because this brought home to me that being a black lawyer within the British legal system would place me in a position where I could get my own experience in my legal career. My diversity would be a positive factor rather than a negative one. Instinctively, I wanted to help, support and protect that 15-year-old. This I believe was the birth of my becoming a social justice champion.

CHAPTER 5

Idyllic Kent Versus Diverse London

I timed my exit from Kent to precision, calculating the day of my qualification as a lawyer in alignment with the three-month notice period. Those three months were filled with pressure from colleagues trying to persuade me to stay, highlighting what a wonderful place the county would be to live in. I can't argue with the fact that Kent is beautiful. The streets were cleaner, and yes, it was a better quality of life than the hustle and bustle of London, with that county's long country lanes and just a short drive to Canterbury or the coast. I could not forget West Malling, where I had my interview, with its picturesque green fields and stone cottages, which would not be out of place in a countryside magazine.

But although things may have changed now, at that time I think Kent lacked diversity, which had always been a problem for me. However, in working in the courts, I was also not naïve to the fact that some parts of Kent were not so affluent, with higher crime rates and poorer living standards. As an owner of a two-bedroom maisonette in London, which was just five minutes from a tube station, it would not have been difficult for me to sell my flat at a reasonable price and buy a lovely flat or even a tiny house in Kent. I would have been able to get a lot more for my money there when compared to soaring property prices in London. As a newly qualified lawyer, my income would also increase, and my travelling expenses would be significantly reduced. Undoubtedly, I had the financial means to make a new life for myself in Kent and have a decent quality of life.

London was just over an hour away, so it would not have been difficult to come to London when I needed to. My parents probably would not have been too happy, but they had always encouraged me to be independent and supported me in the decisions I made. They had travelled thousands of miles to make a new life in a strange country, so it's unlikely they would have had a problem with me being an hour away.

Some black people had decided to move away from London into more idyllic surroundings, but I didn't believe that would have been right for me. Despite the painful incidents in court, I made some great friends in Kent, and when I celebrated my birthday all the legal advisers took me out, and we spent a wonderful evening together. We talked and laughed, and I could see that it would not have been difficult to become a part of their life if I'd stayed. But there was a nagging feeling in my mind that I was getting to a place where I was being accepted. How much of myself would I have lost to compromise the proper version of myself? "Everyone knows Pauline, she's one of us, now." I would become that black person who had managed to mould myself into white society. My culture was significant to me. I was brought up with British and Jamaican roots and was proud of both. But I found the need to dull down the Jamaican aspect of my life while working in Kent, was conscious of that difference between me and my white colleagues. I was terrified that if I'd made the move to Kent, my black heritage would have continued to be eroded until it was no longer significant to me. I didn't want to lose the real me.

I was also alert to the risk I may be taking in moving into an area where I would most likely be on my own as the only black person. I read the horror stories of the racism experienced by Dawn French and Lenny Henry, who had moved to villages outside London, where racists vandalised their cars outside their home with really racist slogans and tried to burn down the couple's house. Dawn French said:

> "It was massively shocking to me. Someone put an oily rag through our front door and tried to burn us down. Luckily, I woke up and smelt it. Otherwise, I'm not sure we would be here."[1]

At one point, the couple had to move police into their home because of the abuse they faced. "I had never experienced anything like that until I met him [Lenny], and I just couldn't believe the continual racism that happens in his life, the casual, insidious racism which I found offensive," Dawn was quoted as saying in the *Daily Express*.[2]

---

1. *Daily Mail* (2014), "Racists tried to torch our home, says Dawn French as she talks of abuse she suffered during her marriage to Lenny Henry," May 19.
2. *Daily Express* (2020), Ingate, Kathryn, "Dawn French and Lenny Henry had to move police officers into home after 'continual racism'," October 12.

Dawn French's admission that she had no understanding of how racism had impacted Lenny Henry until she met him helped to put my feelings about Kent into perspective. In that, my white colleagues, or any future friendships that I may have struck up, however well-meaning, would never be able to understand how it meant to be subjected to racial hatred, in which the problem would only be exacerbated if it invaded what should be the safe space of your home. I would effectively be on my own.

What's interesting is that it appears several black people still feel the same; in 2020, black woman Cephas Williams talked about how she was one of only 2% of black people in Britain living in the countryside, having moved there with her partner. Like me, Cephas had some apprehensions, such as where she would find a quality black hair salon, and worried about missing the rich multiculturalism of London:

> "I am constantly being asked where I am from…on one of my first visits to the local mother-and-baby group, I remember another mother touching my child's hair as if she was petting a dog…"[3]

Cephas described feeling anxious about asking for inclusive books and multicultural themes in her children's classroom, worrying that she might be perceived as the troublemaker parent:

> "Walking into a pub, it's embarrassing to witness the silence and stares, followed by the eruption of talking again once the customers have recovered from the cultural tsunami of having a black woman walk in."[4]

Although Cephas acknowledged that not all white people in the countryside are racist, she went on to say:

> "It's important to understand that ignorant, racist things can come out of the mouths of nice people in Wellington boots. The countryside is a territorial place, full of imperial nostalgia that harks back to a time when black

---

3. *Guardian* (2020), Brown, V V, "To be black in the British countryside means being an outsider," October 20.
4. Ibid.

people were not welcome. The very concept of Britishness is wrapped up in images of the fields of England — and I do not represent that concept."[5]

Considering how adamant I was about returning to London, I seriously considered the prospect of making a new life for myself in Kent. I suppose anyone in my position would have done so because it was an opportunity to change my life. But looking back, I know I made the right decision because I was a Londoner, born and bred, and needed people around me who I could identify with. Therefore, I took my leave of Kent, saying goodbye to my colleagues, who made my last day one to remember.

My desk was covered in balloons and colourful decorations, and they laid on a beautiful spread. My boss and his wife sang a Welsh song at my presentation, which brought me to tears. When I left, my car was overflowing with presents.

If I were to have any doubts about my decision, they would be dispelled years later when a black male friend and I took a drive back into a lovely part of Kent. We drove down country lanes and stopped off in a beautiful area where we enjoyed a picnic, made up of a large bottle of Fanta, cheese, pickle, ham hock sandwiches, and a large packet of salt and vinegar crisps. I reminisced as we drove through West Malling. On our way back, we found a beautiful set of houses. They looked costly, so we decided to take a better look. We stopped at the end of the road and sat silently, taking in our surroundings. We noticed a car pull out from one of the drives and head down the road. I saw two white males in the vehicle as it passed us. As they drove past, they slowed down and looked straight at us both. They moved further down the road, stopped, then turned the car around and parked just a little way behind us. I could see them talking and pointing at us from the rear-view mirror, and they looked angry. But they did not get out of their car.

My friend and I knew that it might be better to move on because the last thing we wanted was to deal with the police. Driving home, I felt disappointed that so little had changed; our glorious day had been tainted by two white males who made it clear we were unwelcome.

---

5. Ibid.

CHAPTER 6

Post Qualification Years

When I left Kent for London, I didn't have a job to return to. I had just enough money to get me through a couple of months. Having recently qualified, I knew I would not simply walk into a job, but it was a chance I was prepared to take. Kent would have happily kept me on as a fully qualified legal adviser. Many trainees choose to stay with the legal firms that have trained them if it is an economically viable option.

I could have followed in the footsteps of several legal advisers who had left the Court Service and joined the CPS, which was a natural progression due to their experience of criminal law and offences, alongside extensive knowledge of how the court ran, which was a great advantage. However, working for the CPS did not appeal to me. At first, I wondered if it was related to my experiences with them during my training contract, but in hindsight it was more related to the work itself, which I got to see first-hand. They were constantly under pressure, sometimes with a mammoth list of cases to get through, and lawyers for the CPS always looked highly stressed. To them, cases were just numbers; they had no time to enjoy the job. I couldn't get to grips with the idea of doing a job that I didn't want, when I had studied and worked so hard to get there. I also knew that as a lawyer I could not be a jack of all trades; I would have to specialise in building my experience and reputation within the legal world.

I signed up with some legal agencies as a newly qualified lawyer. Compared to others I had an impressive CV thanks to my time as a legal adviser, with evidence of extensive training within the courts. Together with my experience as a trained housing benefits officer, dealing with complex Ombudsman complaints. However, a legal job did not fall into my lap, so to survive, I took on short-term agency work as a temporary corporate complaints officer for Southwark Council. The money was great, and it was nice getting back to a decent wage. However when the job became a permanent position and they asked me to apply, I declined. I wanted to work as a lawyer.

On leaving Southwark, I was out of work for about six weeks when a legal agency contacted me about a job that was, in their words "made for me." It was a post for a housing benefits prosecutions lawyer with Hounslow Council. Within minutes of speaking to the principal lawyer, I had secured the job, my first full legal role.

I had no idea how different my life would be as a lawyer. When I met the investigation officers, and they found out about my background, there was a level of respect that I had not had before. I also found that I did not have to compromise who I was; if anything, being authentic attracted more admiration from my colleagues. I enjoyed working in Hounslow, and at first, it was strange sitting on the other side of the magistrates' courts and watching legal advisers doing the job I used to do.

Still, the commute was long and arduous, and the pay was low for my work. When I asked the principal lawyer if there was a chance of a rise because of my experience, she offered me an extra £1 an hour. That's when I decided to look elsewhere. In researching pay for the area of work I was doing, the standard rate was at least £7 more an hour, and I knew my worth. I tried various agencies, including a more prominent one for firms in the City, which clarified that I was not suitable as a candidate and suggested I try elsewhere. The call from Hackney came a couple of weeks later, and on walking back through the doors where I had spent years working as a housing benefits officer, I knew I was home.

I honed my skills as a public sector lawyer, starting in Civil Housing Law as an anti-social behaviour lawyer before moving into the area that would become my specialism: prosecutions. Although this was not the area of law I envisaged for myself, my training within the courts and my local authority experience made it a natural progression. Importantly, I enjoyed working within regulatory enforcement. I had no idea that within just a few years in my role, I would be taken back to the reality of how damaging racism can be.

After three years at Hackney Council, I joined the senior management ranks, having been allowed to obtain an "acting" position within the General Civil Litigation Team. It was an excellent stepping-stone because it enabled me to broaden my skills in civil litigation alongside criminal law and as a lawyer. My team consisted of lawyers and paralegals, who would work on what I like to describe as the miscellaneous work that no-one else wanted to do. This includes debt recovery and leasehold tribunal work, in addition to prosecutions. It was a baptism by fire with a team of ten, but I enjoyed the challenge. Within a year, the team had achieved some great results, and with the support of a fantastic white manager I was content and happy in the role. Therefore, when the permanent senior position was advertised internally, I had no hesitation in applying.

I worked hard on the application and received confirmation that I would be interviewed. I was quietly confident because I knew I could illustrate my team's brilliant results and how I had managed to turn things around with several client departments, who were now happy with how the team was progressing. We also had some great court results. However, I was conscious of the fact that the job was by no means guaranteed, and I would need to give the best interview to secure the permanent position.

On the day of the interview, my team and legal colleagues were incredibly encouraging, telling me to stay calm and just be the best I could be, but as expected, I was pretty nervous. I thought it would be easier because this was an internal position, and I knew the panel was made up of three white members. But if anything, it was more challenging because you can fall into the trap of assuming they know about your achievements. After all, they have worked with you. However, that is something you can never rely on in an interview because the decision can only be based on the answers you give on the day. So, with that in mind, I was determined to provide a detailed response to all the questions.

They smiled and put me at ease on entering the room, explaining the job requirements and what would be expected. I nodded in all the right places and waited for the interview to start. However, I was slightly taken aback when one of the panel members asked me about my legal qualifications and required a detailed account of how I had completed a "full-time" law degree while still working 25 hours a week. I was surprised by the question because I was already a permanent staff member working in an "acting up" position. I had a practising certificate, and the mere fact that I was employed as a lawyer meant that this question bore no relevance to the role.

But as the other panel members allowed the question, I had to spend the first 20 minutes of the interview explaining how a great manager allowed me to effectively arrange my working hours around the university, as long as I could continue working for at least 25 hours a week. I explained how, for three years, my white Cavalier Sri and I made the trip between Hackney and Islington, which resulted in me obtaining a 2:1 law degree. I was then made to talk through my Legal Practice Course and training contract, having to drive back and forth to Kent. As I relayed the information, the panel members looked at me in disbelief, which left me with an uneasy feeling of doubt on their part about my legal journey. But even though I was a little anxious at having to explain myself, I realised, although irrelevant, it indicated how committed I had been to reaching this point in my life and would only show me in a positive light.

The panel member concerned finally allowed the interview to begin. The questions started, which I answered to the best of my ability. However, one question raised a red flag that I could not ignore because, thankfully, it related to a legal point I had prepared a briefing note for just a few weeks before. I smiled and said, "Oh, I prepared a briefing note on this." And the response I received from the panel member was, "Yes, I realised that, but only after I had set the question." Which made it clear that if they had realised I had prepared the briefing note, the question would never have been asked. My paranoia kicked in at this point, but I put it down to my nerves and was still spoiling over the fact that I had wasted so much time justifying how I had qualified.

At the end of the interview, I was still quietly confident. I had answered all the questions, some better than others. Still, I was satisfied that I had given a good account of my achievements and ability to be given the permanent role, having been doing the job for over a year and proving myself capable. I was asked to wait to be recalled as the panel would give me the decision within an hour.

Following the interview, my team and colleagues were optimistic, and although I was still nervous as I awaited their decision, I felt I had done enough to secure the position. I was called back within half-an-hour and asked to sit down. My senior line manager did not look happy, which immediately raised alarm bells, and I listened in shock as the chair of the panel said: "You gave a good interview, but we don't feel that you did well enough for us to offer you the permanent post of a senior lawyer. Therefore, the job is going to be externally advertised. But the good news is that you will not be required to complete another application, as the other external candidates will, and we will automatically interview you. We will arrange for the job to be advertised now and will provide you with the new interview date."

The pain of that moment is hard to describe, but if I were to try and put it into words, all I can say is I was left with a sense of anger, which was so strong that it took me right back into that courtroom in Kent when I had been completely undermined. It wasn't that I didn't get the job; it was the humiliation of facing my team and legal colleagues. What added insult to injury was that they expected me to go through an entire interview and a new set of questions. It was also very likely that I would be the only black woman, pitched against white males, who would have been working in a senior position for a lot longer than I had. I wanted to smash the place because it was so unfair. But, as with the incident in Kent, I nodded, got up, and left the room because, if I'd kicked off, I would have given them exactly what they wanted and lost everything I had worked so hard for.

I sneaked out the back and went for a walk because I needed to clear my head. As soon as the cold air hit, I fell into a flood of tears as I tried to make sense of what had just happened. All I kept thinking was, "What am I going to do? How can I face everyone?" As I cried, I tried to understand why I seemed to take two steps forwards and ten steps back when it came to my legal career.

When I returned and told my team what had happened, they rallied around me and were so angry that I had to calm *them* down. My legal colleagues and the other senior lawyers were bemused and dumbfounded. But I don't know why I was surprised because while in the "acting up" position, I'd witnessed an Asian colleague in a similar role. When the job was advertised they were unsuccessful, and it was offered to a white male. I don't know why I didn't expect the same thing to happen to me.

The next few days were like being in a trance; I didn't have the heart to tell my parents, and I was completely confused about what to do. The atmosphere at work was awful because everyone was upset over what had happened. It also became clear that support was gathering for my dilemma: I had been presented with impossible choices. On the one hand, I could refuse to be re-interviewed and leave the way open for an external candidate to step into the job I had worked so hard at and reap the benefits of my achievements. On the other, I could be re-interviewed. But bearing my previous experience in mind, along with how completely demoralised I was feeling and my loss of confidence in the fairness of the process, I thought it was unlikely that I would get the job in any event. Both options would result in the humiliation of me having to train the new senior they would hire while I took on a subordinate role below them, in full view of my team, my colleagues, and the clients. The final option was that I could leave and walk away from a job I enjoyed, which appeared to be the best option of the three.

I was a proud woman and had taken so much shit, put up with one knock-back after another, but there comes a time that you have to take a stand, legal career or no career because although I am a lawyer, it does not define me. What defines me is what type of person I want to be. I didn't want to rock the boat or be that troublemaker who lodges complaints against management because my job was hard enough without dealing with that. But Dad's advice was never far away. When you're in trouble, think with your head, not your heart. I knew I deserved that job and knew, had I been white, I probably would have been appointed. Although it may have been hard to prove that racism was behind the decision not to appoint me, I was prepared to challenge the decision, which would include the interrogation I was put through about my legal qualifications and how this in itself was strong evidence of unfair bias by the panel member in question. Everyone was behind me, not just behind closed doors but outwardly outspoken about their concerns. My position was also strengthened by my good track record, never having lodged or attracted any complaints before, and being a popular legal team member.

I was in the process of drafting my grievance when something completely unexpected happened. I was called into my line manager's office (he had also been a panel member). He sat me down and presented me with a statement they had drafted. It called out what my manager believed to have been the unfair way I had been treated and how they thought that I would be within my rights to lodge a grievance, which in all likelihood would be successful bearing my exemplary work history in mind. In drafting the statement, my white manager was effectively putting his neck on the line, but he stated he had no choice. He could not accept or agree with the way I had been treated. I seriously considered what my manager was prepared to do, and although I welcomed his support, I could not allow him to risk his career for me. If things escalated to a hearing, my manager would have been called to give evidence, at which point I would be have been happy for him to provide an opinion, but right now, I was ready to stand on my own two feet.

I have no idea what discussions took place behind the scenes, but I do know that a day later I was summoned to the Head of Law's office and informed that they were sorry for any pain or anguish that may have been caused to me. They confirmed that they had decided to withdraw the external advert and formally offer me the permanent senior position. On hearing the news, although somewhat relieved, I didn't jump for joy. I believe they had only decided this because they did not want to be dragged through a grievance or, worse, an employment tribunal. But I figured that in life you may sometimes get a package, and you may not like how it's been wrapped, but all that matters is what's inside.

I didn't want to leave Hackney and start over. I had a good team and was on my way to achieving great things, but this incident and the initial decision not to offer me the position damaged my reputation. It placed me in a difficult position with my Head of Law, who was relatively new at the time, and bearing in mind what had happened, clearly had reservations about my ability. Therefore, over the next few years, I proved that I deserved the position on merit rather than being shooed in via the back door to avoid the scandal of an employment tribunal.

I took nothing for granted, was aggressive and passionate about my job, and was the first one at my desk at six every morning and still there at six at night. Under my leadership, we became an award-winning team. I also became an accredited trainer for Lawyers in Local Government, training lawyers and investigating officers from across the country in prosecutions. On one occasion, I made my way to Oxford, arriving early in order to prepare. I met the organizer, who took me to the room where the training would occur. There was someone already there, a white male, reading a paper. The organizer turned to me and said, "Oh, that's good, at least the trainer has arrived."

"No, I'm the trainer," I told her.

She turned beetroot red and apologised. But instead of anger, I felt frustration that no matter how far I'd come, this stubborn, embedded preconception of my capabilities remained. That day, I took great pleasure in dispelling any doubts anyone had about my ability.

Commenting on a 2023 Black British Voices (BBV) survey,[1] Cynthia Davis CBE, CEO and founder of Diversifying Group, noted that progression for

---

1. Black British Voices (2023), i-Cubed, *The Voice*, University of Cambridge, October.

black employees is notoriously sluggish compared to their white counterparts. In addition, BBV highlighted that where progression does occur, it is viewed with suspicion by others as part of inclusion initiatives. Black employees feel the need to justify their right to be in the room. "I was repeatedly told it just 'wasn't my time' to move up in the organization, only to have to train the underqualified colleague in how to do the job," said Davis.[2]

In considering the findings of the BBV survey and my own experiences, it's frightening how little has changed. But all my experiences within the law and outside have given me an innate sense of justice, one in which I have come to realise that when it comes to equality of treatment, they have no right to ask me to sit on the back of the bus. In 2020 I was able to put this into practice.

---

2. Ibid.

CHAPTER 7

The Black Person's Voice Within the CJS

"It is alleged by some of those who made representations to me that Britain is an institutionally racist society. If by that is meant that it is a society which knowingly, as a matter policy, discriminates against black people, I reject the allegation. If, however, the suggestion being made is that practices may be adopted by public bodies as well as private individuals which are unwittingly discriminatory against black people, then this is an allegation which deserves serious consideration …": Lord Scarman.[1]

It was Summer 2020; everyone was trying to enjoy the warm rays taking us into the beginnings of Autumn whilst doing their best to adhere to social distancing. We were all living in the midst of the Covid-19 pandemic. I had been qualified for a number of years and was a senior lawyer, attending the magistrate's court, where I was representing the local authority on a matter. There was a lot of waiting around before the case was called on. As I sat in the main foyer area, I noticed that there were quite a few black people seated in various areas. But although it was not unusual to see a mixed bag of people from all backgrounds in court, that day was different because I noticed they were families, some young, others old. I knew they were families because of how they referred to each other. Now and again, one of the younger members would get a call, and I could hear them explaining to someone on the other end that they were outside the court and waiting to hear what was happening. It was hard not to eavesdrop because the foyer, although quite packed, was quiet. All of them looked worried and were not saying that much to each other. The air had an eerie feeling. The families would look over at me now and then and I looked back and smiled, but we never spoke.

---

1. Lord Scarman OBE (1981), *The Scarman Report: The Brixton Disorders 10–12 April 1981*, Penguin Books: p. 28.

After waiting for over an hour, the court usher came out and informed me that my case would not be heard until the end of the day because a number of prisoners had been brought in and were waiting in custody. Their cases had to be dealt with first, which made it clear why all the families were there. Of course, I had no idea what those in custody had done and what was happening in relation to their cases. But as a black woman sitting there, it was impossible not to feel something. Crime is not just about the perpetrators; it's also about victims and the families on both sides.

"Oh God, I hope no-one's been killed," I whispered.

During the afternoon, I saw a young white man approach one of the families. They stood up in anticipation and went into the corridor, where they listened intently to the man who was dressed in a suit, carrying a file under his arm, who looked about 25 years old. What struck me at that moment was how this black family were placing their faith in a person who was chasms apart from the world they knew. It cannot be denied that the law is based on evidence, and any lawyer would prepare their case with that in mind, which is not linked to the colour of someone's skin. But no matter how good a lawyer you are, surely it can build trust between you and your client if they believe you have an understanding of the culture, and the world in which they reside. I wanted to get up, go into that corridor, stand beside them, and ask, "Is there anything I can do?" But that was, of course, impossible, and would have been a breach of professional conduct. Therefore, I remained seated and watched as the family returned, and sat back down as the white male left. No matter what your ethnicity, whether you are black or white, court procedure is daunting and complex.

I would hope that for all of us practising law, acting as legal representatives, it is never just about the job, or the black letter of the law. As solicitors, barristers or legal executives we enter people's lives when they become embroiled for whatever reason in the legal system, be it a criminal or a civil matter. Those who come for help and advice look to us to be their voice within the complexities of a world they are unfamiliar with.

We are required to act in the best interests of each client; you must not behave in a way which is likely to diminish the trust and confidence which the public places in you or in the profession. Consider the lack of diversity within the legal profession. Just how easy is it for those who may have little or no knowledge of the "lived experiences" of those clients they represent? Clients look to them as the most important person within the process because they are there to provide that client with a voice.

An excellent example of bringing a lived experience to the table was contained in an interview given by Lord Woolley, a black man born in Leicester in 1961, who was raised on a council estate by his white adoptive parents and later studied Spanish and Politics at Middlesex University. In 1996, he became the co-founder of Operation Black Vote to encourage Britain's black communities to engage themselves in the political process and also highlight concerns within the black community. He was appointed Principal of Homerton College, Cambridge in 2021, and was chair of the UK Government's Disparity Unit. The following year, he was knighted in the Queen's Birthday Honours and then made a life peer. Following his peerage, he stated:

> "I was in the House [of Lords] once and they were talking about identification cards. I said, no, no, because the police will use them, particularly against black kids."

And when he was met with opposition on this point from the Lords he said: "Stop, stop, hands up, members, my Lords and Ladies; how many of you have been stopped and searched by the police? I put my hands up. No-one's moving. I put my hand down." He then asked, "How many of you have been stopped and strip-searched by the police? My hand goes up again, and I heard somebody laugh. I said 'Do you think it's funny? Ask lady Q the young girl if it's funny to be stopped and stripped searched...'" Lord Woolley went on to state, "I have been empowered to speak to that lived experience, in places where that voice isn't heard."[2]

This shows how unique and valuable Lord Woolley's experience is within the Lords because, without it, this perspective would be lost. Which can be parallelled to the point made above regarding the benefit of a legal representative sharing a cultural understanding of their client, or at least having a better understanding of their lived experience. When speaking on their behalf within the justice system, where black voices are in the minority.

---

2. Lord Simon Woolley, Co-Founder, Operation Black Vote, Interview, Goldman Sachs, 8 August 2022. https://www.youtube.com/watch?v=_aLgR9yCpCo

In October 2023, the Black British Voices (BBV) survey found that of the 10,000 black people interviewed, 88% of those surveyed did not trust the CJS.[3] On 5 November 2021, the Bar Council published, "Race at the Bar: A Snapshot Report".[4] Research found that individuals from ethnic minority backgrounds who aspire to be barristers find it harder to secure pupillage (post-qualification training within barristers' chambers) when compared to their similarly qualified white British peers. However, only 1% of judges are black 2% are from mixed ethnic backgrounds and 5% of from an Asian background. Barristers from black, Asian, and other ethnic minority backgrounds can feel hyper-visible, bullied, harassed, and marginalised at work, especially at court.[5]

In 2017, barrister Mary Aspinall-Miles criticised judges who "belittle and undermine" advocates, claiming they can profoundly impact wellbeing. In a Twitter post, the barrister said she had seen judges come across as "unnecessarily aggressive/sharp" over small issues. "Their criticisms in that tone sting and undermine professional confidence. The words stay with me long after the case is done," she said, adding that she and other barristers had occasionally been spoken to in a tone that would make most people have "employment lawyers on speed dial." Aspinall-Miles continued:

> "You won't improve advocacy or performance by undermining and belittling advocates or welding yourself to an old view of the job. What happens when a relatively junior member of bar comes into contact like that? I am still smarting at something that was said to me without foundation from over ten days ago and I bet I am not alone in these things. We need honesty in these things if we are truly to achieve wellbeing at the bar … I have no issue being brought to task by a judge for shortcomings/failings, in fact I welcome it if it helps me improve, but the tone is key."[6]

Does it make a difference that Mary Aspinall-Miles is a white barrister? No. Because I am sure, a number of solicitors and barristers alike can relay horror

---

3. Black British Voices: "i-Cubed" (2023), *The Voice*, University of Cambridge.
4. "Race at the Bar: A Snapshot Report." https://www.barcouncil.org.uk/uploads/assets/d821c952-ec38-41b2-a41ebeea362b28e5/Race-at-the-Bar-Report-2021.pdf (accessed 29 January 2022).
5. Ibid.
6. Walters, Max (2017), "Barrister Lifts Lid on Impact of Rude and Aggressive Judges," *Law Society Gazette*, 12 October. https://www.lawgazette.co.uk/law/barrister-lifts-lid-on-impact-of-rude-and-aggressive-judges/5063182.article (accessed 29 January 2022).

stories of how they have been lambasted by judges in open court, which is being dealt with, but in my case, spending 20 minutes standing to my feet being laid into by a judge, in front of my clients was not only unpleasant it was uncalled for. Particularly when, at the end of it, I was able to provide proof that it was indeed the court that was at fault. The fact that I was nervous about having to show the judge that they were incorrect in their assumption emphasised the power they wield in court.

But as Dr Leary stated earlier, there is a distinct difference between living in the skin of a white barrister or solicitor to that of living in the skin of a black solicitor or barrister. There are those within the profession who are reluctant to accept this distinction.

In 2020, Leslie Thomas a high-profile black QC (now KC), and first Professor of Law at Gresham College, said: "Barristers who believe their chambers are 'colour-blind' and treat everyone the same 'have a problem' and need to change their mindset." Adding,

> "Racism and discriminatory behaviours pervade all levels of society, and our legal system is not immune from the same. I have experienced it many times in my career. One judge said to me, 'Mr Thomas, in this country we do things in this way…Just think about it: if I can be treated in this way and I am a member of a well-respected profession, it takes very little imagination to think how black defendants are treated."[7]

In 2017, David Lammy MP released the Lammy Review, which considered racial bias throughout the CJS.[8] The British legal system is enshrined within what is known as the Rule of Law. Central to this rule is the concept that citizens should be equally treated before the law and that "no man is above the

---

7. Rose, Neil (2024), "Your chambers aren't colour blind, top QC tells barristers," *Legal Futures*, 22 June. https://www.legalfutures.co.uk/latest-news/your-chambers-arent-colour-blind-top-qc-tells-barristers (accessed 8 January 2024).
8. The Lammy Review (2017), "An Independent Review into the Treatment of, and Outcomes for, Black, Asian and Minority Ethnic Individuals in the Criminal Justice System," 8 September.

law."[9] It's also crucial that within the rule, citizens are able to access the courts and be heard by independent judges.[10]

The Lammy Review stated that to build trust and respect for the Rule of Law, there must be a step change in the magistracy and especially with judges, arguing that until this is achieved, there will continue to be a sense of "them and us" among black and minority defendants.[11]

In November 2022, the report "Racial Bias and the Bench" was published by the University of Manchester in response to the Judicial Diversity and Inclusion Strategy (2020–2025).[12] It explored and evaluated racial bias, as well as anti-racism, among judicial office holders (judges). Drawing on the findings of 373 legal professionals as well as existing research, it evaluated the racial fairness of judges and racial guidance and diversity initiatives. The ethnicity of those who provided observations was 13% Asian, 14% black, 12% mixed, 4% other, 1% preferred-not-to-say, and 56% white.[13] Within the report it was found that 55.6% of legal professionals said that they had witnessed one or more judges act with racial bias in their treatment of defendants.[14]

Many respondents suggested that a key way in which judicial racial bias is communicated is non-verbal, through tone of voice, demeanour, and body language, which suggests a relative lack of respect towards ethnic minority people in court proceedings. Hence:

"Judges play a powerful role of modelling normative courtroom attitudes and behaviour; if they adopt a disparaging and distrustful manner towards

---

9. Dicey, A V (1915), *Introduction to the Study of the Law of the Constitution*, MacMillan and Co Ltd, p. 189.
10. James, Lisa, Zyl Smit, Jan Van, (2022), "The Rule of Law: What It Is and Why Does it Matter?," The Constitution Unit, 15 December. https://constitution-unit.com/2022/12/15/the-rule-of-law-what-is-it-and-why-does-it-matter/ (accessed 6 January 2024).
11. The Lammy Review (2017), "An Independent Review into the Treatment of, and Outcomes For, Black, Asian and Minority Ethnic Individuals in the Criminal Justice System", p. 31 Also see Ministry of Justice (2016), "Black, Asian and Minority Ethnic Disproportionately in the Criminal Justice System in England and Wales", p. 27.
12. Monteith, Keir KC, Professor Quinn, Eithne, Professor Dennis, Andrea L, Dr Joseph Sailsbury, Remi, Kane, Erica, Addo, Franklyn, Professor McGourlay (2022), "Racial Bias and the Bench: A Response to the Judicial Diversity and Inclusion Strategy (2020–2025)," Manchester University.
13. Ibid: 10.
14. Ibid: 15–16.

people of colour then many others in the courtroom will likely pick up on and reproduce unthinkingly."[15]

This point is an important one when considering my own experience. I was acting for the prosecution, in which an application made by the local authority was being challenged. During my cross-examination of a witness, I noticed the judge give a discreet smile to my legal counterpart, who was acting for the defence, who in turn smiled back. The decision ultimately went against me, but the ruling itself did not hurt as much as that "secret smile" between two white males in a courtroom, in which I was the only black person present. As stated by the report, that subtle smile and how it made me feel, knocked my confidence and, rightly or wrongly, gave me the impression that the case would not go my way.

The report found that there is so little scrutiny of judicial bias, some might have concluded that the problem simply resides with ethnic minority people themselves and not the justice system, therefore no further action is needed.[16] But I do not agree, because although everyone witnessed what happened in court that day, I was the only one who was impacted by it. Which only reaffirms how dangerous the subtlety of racial judicial bias can be.

---

15. Ibid: 13.
16. Ibid: 19.

CHAPTER 8

The Mangrove Nine

Confronting any unfair treatment is never easy, and as a black person complaining against a large powerful organization, such as the police, it is even more daunting. But it's important that black people along with the rest of society are given the opportunity to exert that right. On 1 September 1968, the *Observer*, in an article entitled "Police Brush Up Their Race Relations,"[1] reported that police were complaining that discrimination was working in favour of immigrants because policemen were fearful of complaints. Such concerns, however, were not based on facts. Figures for complaints by black people against Metropolitan Police officers from the 1 April 1962 to the 31 March 1963 revealed that of 122 complaints, only six were substantiated and upheld.[2] General complaint figures for 1968 showed that of 909 allegations of offences committed by Metropolitan Police officers, excluding traffic offences, 12 (a mere 1.3%) were substantiated.[3] In the case of specific allegations of racial discrimination by such officers for 1969, of 41 complaints, none were substantiated.[4]

It was on the back of these statistics, coupled with the turbulent relationship between the police and the black community, that on 9 August 1970, a group of Black Power activists led 150 people on a march against police harassment of the black community in Notting Hill, London. They called for the "end of the persecution of the Mangrove Restaurant" based in Notting Hill. Between January 1969 and July 1970, the police raided the Mangrove Restaurant 12 times. No evidence of illegal activity was found during these raids.

---

1. James Whitfield (2003): "The Metropolitan Police: Alienation, Culture, and Relations with London's Caribbean Community (1950–1970)," *Crime, Histoire and Sociétés /Crime, History and Societies*, Vol. 7, No. 2, Varia.
2. PRO (report of figures in relation to complaints) MEPO2/9854.
3. PRO MEPO2/10790.
4. PRO MEPO2/10791.

Local Police Constable Frank Pulley remained convinced that the restaurant was a den of iniquity frequented by "pimps, prostitutes, and criminals."[5] At the 1970 march in defence of the Mangrove, violence broke out between the police and protestors.

On 5 October 1971, nine men and women were put on trial at the Old Bailey for causing a riot at the march. They were Darcus Howe, Frank Crichlow, Rhodan Gordon, Althea Jones-Lecointe, Barbara Beese, Godfrey Miller, Rupert Glasgow Boyce, Anthony Carlisle Innis, and Rothwell Kentish. These men and women became known nationally as the Mangrove Nine.[6]

The trial was significant in that, firstly, Jones-Lecointe and Howe opted to defend themselves so that they could accurately express to the court the experiences of black people, particularly concerning unjust treatment by the police, but also their broader social experience.[7] Secondly, they demanded that the trial be heard by an all-black jury, applying rights enshrined within Magna Carta to trial by one's peers, which Judge Edward Clarke rejected. However, the judge did allow the defence the right to challenge who would sit on the jury, which resulted in the defence dismissing 63 potential jurors, that led to two black people gaining a place on the 12 person jury.

As I read about the Mangrove Nine, I recalled how I had witnessed police officers stop and search my 12-year-old brother on his way home from school, making him open his school bag and empty the pockets of his school blazer just a few doors away from our home. I was not opposed to an all-black jury because, like Lord Woolley, I felt they could bring their invaluable experience. However, as a trained lawyer, I had a different perspective, coming down on the side of the judge, who I believe was correct in refusing the defendant's request for such a jury. Why? One of the rationales for trial by jury is that the defendant's conduct is assessed according to local norms of 12 ordinary people whose outlooks have been moulded by their diverse characters, histories, and lifestyles. Although it has been determined that the court recognises that a juror may draw inspiration from his or her past,[8] the law does not want

---

5. Constable Frank Pulley quoted in "A Den of Iniquity," *Kensington Post*, 12 October 1971, as cited in Rob Waters (2019), *Thinking Black: Britain, 1964–1985*: 99

6. *DPP v Innis, Kentish, Gordon and Others* (1971): see https://www.nationalarchives.gov.uk/education/resources/mangrove-nine-protest/

7. Dr Andrew Gilbert (2021), "The Mangrove Nine: Fifty Years On," Open University.

8. *R v Smith (Lance)* [2003] EWCA Crim 283, [2003] 1 WLR 2229: 37; *R v M* [2004] EWCA Crim 1610: 15–16.

jurors to consider extra-evidential factors that are likely to cause a miscarriage of justice.[9] Amongst these factors is reliance on negative[10] racial stereotypes, such as to dismiss self-defence because those with dark skin are believed to be inclined to aggression.[11]

I could not help thinking that it would be equally dangerous for an all-black jury, who could similarly be influenced by extra-evidential factors not related to the evidence itself. Particularly if they have had bad experiences with the police or experienced racism within their everyday working lives. Therefore, I felt that a diverse jury, comprised of both black and white people, could act as a deterrent for jury members on both sides, who may harbour thoughts of negative stereotypes, both racial and in how they perceive the police. I was also convinced that if an all-black jury were to find the defendants not guilty, then this could result in the assumption that the verdict was biased and would lack credibility. In addition, black people are a part of British society, and we have fought for the right to be accepted as equal citizens within Britain. Therefore, by requesting an all-black jury, we would be effectively segregating ourselves from the very society in which we reside, which could lead to further resentment.

More importantly, although our jury system is centuries old, successive studies show that, on average, jury verdicts are not affected by ethnicity.[12] A detailed study of verdicts across England and Wales, published in 2010, found that black and ethnic minority and white defendants were convicted at very similar rates, including in cases with all-white juries.[13] The 2010 study was updated in 2017 to inform the in-depth Lammy Review, which conducted extensive investigations into the CJS. It analysed over 390,000 jury decisions between 2006 and 2014 and found that jury conviction rates were similar across different ethnic groups.[14] This is important because black people are underrepresented within

---

9. The dividing line between "acceptable ordinary differences in expectations and reactions based on experience, and unacceptable prejudice or bias" is of course problematic: Ellis and Diamond, "Race Diversity and Jury Composition," 1035.
10. A positive stereotype might cause justice to miscarry if it leads jurors to trust an untrustworthy witness.
11. Kalunta-Crumpton, A (1999), *Race and Drug Trials*, ebook 2018, Routledge Revivals.
12. "Independent Review into the Treatment of, and outcomes for Black, Asian and Minority Ethnic Individuals in the Criminal Justice System" (Lammy Review) (2017); Thomas, C (2010), "Are Juries Fair?", Ministry of Justice Research Series; and Thomas C (2017), "Ethnicity and Fairness of Jury Trials in England and Wales 2006–2014" (2017), *Criminal Law Review*, No. 9.
13. Thomas C (2010), "Are Juries Fair?": see within previous footnote.
14. Ibid.

the legal system. Still, as they form a cross-section of society, they must have the opportunity to use their voices in judging their peers.

After a trial lasting 55 days and jury deliberation of more than eight hours, all defendants were cleared of the main charge of inciting a riot. Rupert Boyce, Rhodan Gordon, Anthony Innis and Altheia Jones-Lecointe received suspended sentences for lesser offences, including affray and assaulting police officers.

What is also of crucial significance in his summing up at the end of the trial was that Judge Clarke noted that the prosecution had "regrettably shown evidence of racial hatred on both sides."[15] This was the first judicial recognition of institutional racism in the Metropolitan Police. However, there was an acknowledgement by the judge of racial hatred on the part of the police for the first time in their treatment of the black protestors. It doesn't sit well with me that he determined that black people could be seen as having acted in a racist way towards the police. The relationship between the black community and the police was strained, and animosity existed between them. Still, it could have been argued that the black community was reacting to its treatment at the hands of the police from a social justice perspective rather than a racial one.

On Christmas Eve 1971, a senior police officer wrote an internal memo stating that the judge's comments were "quite uncalled for."[16] On the 31 January 1972, the Assistant Commissioner wrote a letter to the Director of Public Prosecutions (DPP) which stated:

> "…the officer in the case makes reference to certain remarks made by the learned judge, and he expresses the opinion that the observations by Judge Edward Clarke were unjustified so far as the police witnesses are concerned…they have caused concern to senior officers of the force. It is thought…without further qualification, the remarks may well be quoted for some time to come by persons who wish to infer racial hatred exists amongst officers of this force."[17]

---

15. Mangrove Nine Protest, National Archives: https://www.nationalarchives.gov.uk/education/resources/mangrove-nine-protest/
16. Gilbert, Dr Andrew (2021), "The Mangrove Nine: Fifty Years On," Open University.
17. Ibid, Letter from Assistant Commissioner to DPP, 31 January 1972 (MEPO 31/20).

The DPP refused to approach the judge, as the Home Secretary was looking into it.[18] Furthermore, Parliamentary archives reveal that in January 1972, then Home Secretary Reginald Maudling MP, requested Judge Clarke to clarify his views.[19]

On 27 January 1972, Maudling was presented with several questions in Parliament, one of which came from Bruce Douglas-Mann MP, who said:

> "…the acquittals in the Mangrove case raise a strong inference that several police officers were lying in concert and that, with the connivance of senior officers, they have been responsible for persecution of particularly articulate black people in the area…only…an inquiry will clear the imputations which have been raised against the police officers concerned."[20]

In response, Maudling said: "I do not in any way accept the imputations based on the result of that particular case."[21] In reflecting on the Mangrove trial, Ian MacDonald (barrister for Barbara Beese) wrote:

> "The Mangrove Nine trial was a watershed because we learned through experience how to confront the power of the court because the defendants refused to play the role of 'victim' and rely on the so-called 'expertise' of the lawyer. Once you recognise the defendant as a self-assertive human being, everything in the court has to change. The power and role of lawyers—the advocacy and the case preparation."[22]

Judge Clarke's statement was never withdrawn. Twenty-eight years after the Mangrove trial, Sir William Macpherson, a retired High Court judge, led the public inquiry into the murder of Stephen Lawrence. In February 1999, based

---

18. Ibid, Letter from Assistant Commissioner to DPP, 25 February 1972 (MEPO 31/20).
19. Minister's case: Rt Hon Reginald Maudling MP to His Honour Judge Edward Clarke QC; HO 325/144 1972 Jan 01–1972 Dec 31.
20. Community Relations (Notting Hill) (1972), *Hansard*, House of Commons (HC Deb 27 January, Col 829, cc1600–2 Co).
21. Ibid.
22. Thompson, Ife (2020), "Black Lives Matter UK: For Lasting Change, We Need Movement Lawyers," *Each Other*, 3 August (Retrieved 15 November 2020); Gilbert, Dr Andrew (2021) "The Mangrove Nine: Fifty Years On," Open University; MacDonald, I (1977); "Up Against the Lawyers" in Field P, Bunce R, Hassan L, and Peacock, M (eds.) (2019), *Here to Stay, Here to Fight: A "Race Today" Anthology*, London: Pluto Press: pp. 154–7.

on the evidence before him, found the police response to the teenager's killing, to be "institutionally racist."[23]

Reading about the Mangrove Nine was incredibly influential in demonstrating how important it was to use our voice within the courtroom and every aspect of our lives. It also showed how strong black voices could be used in the fight for justice, which I wanted to be a part of. It seemed everywhere I turned, I was being guided in a specific direction, far away from the prosecution work in which I had specialised. The key was that I had to have an open mind about what lay ahead because it was impossible to ignore the urge towards the world of social justice.

---

23. "Report of an Inquiry by Sir William MacPherson" presented to Parliament, February 1999.

CHAPTER 9

The Black Queen, Margaret Thatcher and the Angry Black Woman

My conversation with Dr Agnes Kaposi helped me recognise how important it was to be the best I could be in all my endeavours. But it's equally crucial that my achievements receive appropriate recognition. This is not an egotistical ride. I want to build respect among those in and outside my profession based on being good at what I do, not because I am black.

Nevertheless, I've found that when it comes to successes and accomplishments, there is an ongoing reluctance to distinguish between the person and the colour of their skin. It manifests itself in many ways, including the negative perceptions attached to the black woman. An example of this relates to the look of surprise on people's faces when they see me for the first time. I am regularly greeted with the words, "Oh, you're Pauline Campbell." My accent and name do not indicate that I could be black, and if I issue correspondence and speak to people on the phone before a face-to-face meeting, the reaction is always the same when I walk into the room. In addition, I am always on guard about how I react in a situation, because when it comes to a black woman, assertiveness is mistaken for aggression, which is incredibly frustrating.

In 1993, the Italian company Benetton released one of its most controversial advertising campaigns in which they turned the former Monarch, Queen Elizabeth II, into a black woman. The image of a dark-skinned Elizabeth with African-American facial features and black hair was originally published in the fourth issue of Colors (the Benetton house magazine), in 1993 which was entirely devoted to race and entitled "What if…?"[1]

At the time, Benetton's company communications director Peter Fressola stated, "British tabloids went wild." The newspaper headlines accompanying

1. *Colors* (1993), What If…?, Benetton (Editor in Chief Tibor Kalman).

the Queen's photo included: "We Are Not Amused" and "Mam'y."[2] Mam'y, also known as Mammy, was created during slavery in America to produce the false perception that blacks, in this case, black women, were contented, even happy, as slaves. With a wide grin, hearty laughter, and loyal servitude, the Mammy figure was offered as evidence of the supposed humanity of the institution of slavery. Mammys were portrayed as obese, coarse, maternal figures.[3]

There is little doubt that the royals, now with Charles III at the helm, are fiercely guarded by British royalists. When they saw the late Queen, who for them was the symbol of the royal establishment and patriotism, portrayed as a black woman, they were outraged and the Benetton photo was met with staunch retaliation. Fressola stated that some of the company's stores in Great Britain were painted black, with signs indicating, "If you can make the Queen black, we can do the same to your stores."[4]

Although the image of the Black Queen took centre stage in stirring up controversy, images also featured a Chinese-looking Pope, a white Michael Jackson, a blue-eyed Spike Lee, and a black Arnold Schwarzenegger. Fressola stated in relation to the "What if … ?" campaign, "The idea is consistent with our celebration of diversity, our concept of raising issues. The whole magazine is based on race and racism, and we are simply asking, 'What if all our racial preconceptions were flipped around?'"[5]

In November 2015, Francesco Bonami, Oliviero Toscani and Luciano Benetton released the book, *"COLORS": A Book About a Magazine About the Rest of the World*. It aimed to explore the best of visual and textual material of 90 issues of the magazine, created by the photographer Oliviero Toscani and art director Tibor Kalman, in 1991. In 2015, a review of this book written by writer and editor, Madeleine Morley suggested that the New Zealand Government stopped an image from appearing in the book, stating, "The only thing Damiani [the publisher] wasn't able to print was the image they consider the most iconic and recognisable in the universe of COLORS. The picture of the British Queen with black skin." According to the concept, editing, art directors

2. Buck, Genevieve (1993), "Leave it to Benetton to Question a Black-and-White Issue," *Chicago Tribune*, 14 April.
3. Ferris State University, Jim Crow Museum of Racist Memorabilia. https://www.ferris.edu/jimcrow/mammies/ (accessed 6 June 2020).
4. Buck, Genevieve (1993): see earlier footnote.
5. Ibid.

and designers, Sebastiano Mastroeni, Alessandro Cavallini, Andrea Cavallini the New Zealand Government did not allow publication.[6] In an article about the censoring of the Queen's image author and art critic Lana Lopesi found the Queen "quite beautiful in her new ethnicity, and even now I admit that it makes my subversive heart sing to see her represented so."[7]

As a black woman, I was left with an uneasiness at such consternation about the Queen of England being black, even through the eyes of fictitious imagery. The Queen had been in my life, all my life, she was a constant, and every Christmas Day Mum would quieten us down, and get Dad to turn off his reggae music, so that she could listen to the Queen's Speech. As a British citizen it made no sense that people were so angry, because love her of hate her, the Queen was a representation of British society, which included black and white people. Britain was a part of the Commonwealth and celebrated that fact. Therefore, I couldn't understand why this was so shocking to them. What this once again illustrates is how blind racism continues to rear its ugly head. Considering Lana Lopesi's reference to some form of rebellion, or insubordination for deeming the black image of the Queen "quite beautiful" also left me astonished, because it appeared people had missed the point.

Elizabeth II could arguably be described by my generation as a symbol. Her reign began on the 6 February 1952, and her coronation took place on the 2 June 1953, when she was just 27 years old, following the death of her father, King George VI. She saw 14 prime ministers during her reign, which started with Conservative Winston Churchill and ended with Conservative Liz Truss. On 9 September 2015, Elizabeth II became the longest reigning Monarch, having surpassed the previous record set by her great-great-grandmother, Queen Victoria. At the time of her death in 2022 she had reigned for 70 years.

What would happen if one day, the Queen had woken up and by some twist of fate, or divine intervention, call it what you will, she was suddenly, black? The question is controversial, and it is hardly feasible to think this could have ever happened. But, what if in some stretch of the imagination it did happen? Would the fact that her skin colour had changed overnight take away everything she had achieved and represented in her 70-year reign? The categorical

---

6.   Lopesi, Lana (2016), "Censoring Colors: Did the New Zealand Government Stop a Famous Image of Queen Elizabeth From Being Published?" See https://designassembly.org.nz/2018/03/23/censoring-colour/
7.   Ibid.

answer is a resounding No! Therefore, those loyal subjects who levied ridicule and daubed black paint over Benetton's stores after the creation of The Black Queen were effectively telling the Queen that they loved and revered everything she stood for, but it was only on the proviso that it came on condition that she was white.

I wish I could say we have come a long way since 1993. But have we? Nicknamed the Iron Lady of the Western World by a Russian journalist, Margaret Thatcher was Prime Minister for eleven years and 288 days, making her the longest-serving holder of that off of modern times. Under Thatcherism, she took on the might of the unions during the miners' strike of 1984–85, which was a defining moment in the history of British coal mining, and the most significant industrial dispute in post-war Britain. It pitted thousands of miners and their trade unions against her and her Conservative Government, which supported plans to shut 20 coal pits. About three-quarters of the country's 187,000 miners went on strike to oppose the pit closures, expected to mean 20,000 job losses. Thousands of officers were drafted to police the picket lines, with violence breaking out at times. The miners' eventual defeat ended an era for Britain's trade union movement and helped cement Mrs Thatcher's reputation as the Iron Lady. It paved the way for privatising more nationalised industries and utilities, including steel, railways, gas, telecoms, and water.[8]

Historians describe her as powerful, assertive, self-assured, and confident. But in posing the same question with respect to the Black Queen, what would have happened if Margaret Thatcher had gone to bed and woken up a black woman? Would her Iron Lady's positive, assertive qualities suddenly have flipped into those of an angry black woman?

"The idea that you can be a voice for the voiceless is still very important": Diane Abbott.[9]

In 1987, Diane Abbott became the first black woman elected to Parliament and is still the longest-serving black MP. Despite her parents leaving school at

---

8. Morris, Georgina (2008), "Miners' Strike 1984: Why UK Miners Walked Out and How it Ended," BBC England, 2 March. https://www.bbc.co.uk/news/uk-england-68244762#:~:text=The%20miners'%20strike%20of%201984,to%20shut%2020%20coal%20pits.

9. Iqbal, Nosheen, Interview with Diane Abbott, (British) *Vogue*, 15 March 2024.

fourteen, Abbott studied history at Cambridge University. During her career, she worked tirelessly to support black women and children and address the causes of educational underachievement of London's black pupils. In 2008 Abbott's speech on the Counter Terrorism Bill won the Parliamentary Speech of the Year Award from *Spectator* magazine.[10] However, despite over 30 years in politics, in 2017, in the run-up to a general elections, Amnesty International revealed that Abbott alone received almost half of all abusive tweets sent to female MPs, 45% in the six weeks before election day, receiving hundreds every day. Abbott stated, "It's the volume of it which makes it so debilitating, corrosive, and upsetting."[11]

Not only did Diane Abbott top the list of MPs for the most significant number of abusive tweets received, but she received ten times more abuse than any other woman MP in the run-up to that election and eight times more abuse than any other woman MP during the period of the analysis. Amnesty's research also found that black women MPs were found to receive 2,781 abusive tweets per MP. Still, when Diane Abbott was excluded from the analysis, it revealed that black women MPs received 81 abusive tweets per MP.[12]

In March 2024, it was revealed that West Yorkshire Police were investigating "racist comments which were allegedly made at a meeting" by Conservative donor Frank Hester in 2019, who told colleagues (and later apologised) that looking at Diane Abbott made you "want to hate all black women" and that she "should be shot."[13]

As a woman working in a white male-dominated world, women from all backgrounds learn to grow a thicker skin to wrap themselves as armour to protect them against the misogynistic insults that are an unwelcome aspect of their professional lives. Notably, even Margaret Thatcher stated as late as 1970, "There will not be a woman Prime Minister in my lifetime—the male population are too prejudiced."[14]

10. Hoskin, Peter (2008), *The Spectator*, 13 November. https://www.spectator.co.uk/article/spectator-threadneedle-parliamentarian-award-winners/
11. "Diane Abbott talks about 'sheer levels of hatred' she receives online," Amnesty International UK, Press release, 6 September 2017.
12. Ibid.
13. Mason, Rowena (2024), "Police investigate alleged racist remarks by Frank Hester," *Guardian*, 22 March.
14. Sandbrook, Dominic (2013), Viewpoint, "What if Margaret Thatcher had never been?," *BBC News Magazine*, April 9.

Thatcher and Abbott may come from different cultural backgrounds, but both had to fight for their place in the political world, dominated by white males. The question is, "Why is one revered while the other is ridiculed?" I would argue that holding your own as a woman within the political world or any profession is commendable no matter what colour you are. When it comes to success, being assertive, and standing your ground, we are all Iron Ladies.

CHAPTER 10

My First Brush with Windrush

It was a Thursday in the spring of 2018 just past 6 am, and I was the first one in. Doing a 12-hour day had become a way of life for me as a senior lawyer because running a busy legal team required that I put in the hours. I also found that my day was more productive the earlier I arrived, as I could get a lot more work done between 6 and 9 am to make the most of those precious three hours. That morning I was approached by a Jamaican-born agency staff member working as a contract worker for the council for a few years. The person did not work for Legal, but we spoke regularly in the mornings, which was nice, so daily morning chats became a welcome addition to my day. That day, the person approached me and said they needed my help. On taking them into our Library Room, they broke down in tears, stating that although they had lived and worked in Britain for several years, their contractor had informed them that day that they would need to leave work and could not return until their documentation had been checked and verified.

I had no idea what this entailed because, to tell the truth, I could not understand why this was a problem as the person had worked in Britain with settled status for several years. However, I agreed to call the contractors on their behalf, who confirmed that, as employers, they were required to check the person's right to work. Even though they had received updated papers, the person was prohibited from working until further checks had been conducted, which their employers envisaged would take approximately six weeks. I explained that the person needed to work, but they insisted they could do nothing. They assured me that the papers submitted were sufficient, but they needed to conduct appropriate checks. I was bemused and frustrated, trying to make the contractor understand that, if the documents were in order, I could not understand why the worker was prohibited from earning a wage. Still, they were adamant that a process must be followed because failure to do so could result in a fine of up to £10,000.

I relayed the information to the worker, who told me that, thankfully, they had some money saved, to wait until they were allowed to return to work. At the end of the call, the person broke down because they were terrified that this was connected to their right to remain in Britain. I tried to reassure them that they had nothing to worry about in that respect. I advised that if they encountered any problems, several agencies, Citizens' Advice, and other organizations specialising in these areas could help. I also agreed that I would help in any way I could, such as drafting letters or speaking on their behalf, if need be. I provided my number so they could call in the event of an emergency. But all day, I could not get the feeling of utter frustration and anger out of my mind as I had to watch the innocent and lovely worker walk out the door, knowing they could not return until their papers had been verified.

I was on tenterhooks for the next few weeks, watching the door every morning to see if they would return. Finally, after four or five weeks, the worker was there. I breathed a sigh of relief when they returned to work and confirmed everything was okay and they had been permitted to return to work. But what astounded me about this person was they had lived in the UK for several years, having arrived from Jamaica. All of their papers were in order, there was no question of their right to reside in the UK, yet their authentic documents had to be checked and re-checked, resulting in them being unable to work for several weeks, with nothing in place to support them.

But importantly, it was how I felt as a lawyer trying to comfort this person in their distress. This was by no means the first time I had assisted someone who had reached out to me for help. People would regularly approach me and request that I help them draft letters to their child's school, deal with debt matters, and with various landlord issues. It had become a way of life for me, which I enjoyed doing, all free of charge, because it was the right thing to do and because many of the people who approached me were Jamaican, and we had a cultural bond; they trusted me. But this was my first experience of someone being caught up in a possible Windrush scenario, which helped bring the scandal's horrors alive. What if something had gone wrong? If an official had decided they were not happy with the papers submitted? That would have ended this person's right to work and plunged them into poverty and even homelessness.

All this occurred around the same time that stories began to break about others trapped in what became known as the "hostile environment". A phrase coined by former Home Secretary Theresa May in May 2012, when she delivered her hard line stance on immigration in an interview with the *Telegraph*, saying, "The aim is to create here in Britain a hostile environment for illegal migration."[1] A speech that planted the seedlings for the beginning of the Windrush Scandal. In her speech at the Conservative Party Conference in 2015, May warned that "millions" of people wanted to migrate to the UK. She said Britain should focus on aid rather than helping refugees who had travelled to Europe. She repeated claims that immigration pushed down wages. She blamed unemployment, the housing crisis, and underinvestment in schools on immigration, making it clear she intended to push on with controlling immigration and justifying the need for further immigration controls. These controls, incorporated into the 2014 and 2016 Immigration Acts, effectively made immigration enforcement officers out of a range of citizens and organizations, from council workers to landlords, who were being required to conduct right-to-rent checks, to doctors assessing the immigration status of the sick before they were treated. Bank checks, driving licence checks, and employment checks were demanded. Immigration controls were effectively introduced to all walks of life.

Albert Thompson (who asked for his real name to be removed) had been living in the UK for 44–45 years and had worked since 1974, paid his national insurance and always paid his taxes. In 2017, Albert visited his GP for a check-up and had blood tests taken. The results revealed he had prostate cancer. Albert thought the hospital would take him in and start administering treatment at the Royal Marsden. However, on his arrival, Albert said:

> "One of the nurses didn't even take me into a room, just in the walkway, and she was talking to me, and she says, if I cannot produce a passport or visa, then I have to pay. First, she says £53,000, and then she says £54,000. I felt like I was going to pass out. I said £54,000. I don't have it. Not even 54 pence."[2]

1. "We're going to give illegal migrants a really hostile reception," Theresa May interview, James Kirkup and Robert Winnett, *Telegraph*, 25 May 2012.
2. Windrush Scandal: "Albert Thompson on his £54,000 cancer bill," Ekaterine Ochagavia, Maeve Shearlaw, Mustafa Khalili, and Amelia Gentleman, *Guardian*, 19 April 2018.

Albert went to the immigration office to see if they could find any paperwork so he could obtain a passport, but they stated they couldn't find any trace of him, and his work and pensions had nothing on him either.

Albert worked in the UK until 27 February 2006; he had since 1974.

> "I'm trying to get help at the moment and get my passport sorted out, but it ain't going to happen overnight. At present, the NHS has left me in Limbo. Like I say, probably to die…I don't know what's going on inside, and that's worrying. I keep getting extra pain that I never had before. I get a bit depressed, stressed out, and anxious. That was it."[3]

At the time, a spokesperson for the Royal Marsden NHS Foundation Trust said: "We follow the same guidance for all patients to ensure fair and equal access to NHS services. We are sorry we have caused Mr Thompson distress and uncertainty and are working hard to resolve this as quickly as possible."[4]

When I read Albert's story written by *Guardian* journalist Amelia Gentlemen, the lawyer in me thought, "That can't be right." Legally, something must have gone wrong. Albert had been in Britain for over 45 years and had paid his taxes and national insurance for over 30 years. I was no expert in tax law, but I located details that confirmed that the NHS England budget, including things like hospitals, public health initiatives, and so on, are mainly paid for through general taxation and national insurance contributions from employees, employers, and the self-employed, in which Albert was included.[5]

Albert's story, alongside that of the person whose papers were questioned at work, intrigued me. I wanted to know more about what legal rule allowed the hospital the right to deny Albert's treatment because, although I was aware that others were already looking into this, I had to find out for myself what could have gone wrong in his case. Dad had passed away a few years before, in 2013, and had spent the last days of his life in a hospital. We all expected him to come home, and when he died, it was a shock to us all. But I will never forget the kindness of the nurses who cared for him during that time, and it is hard to imagine what would have happened if he had been refused that right,

---

3. Ibid.
4. Ibid.
5. How is the NHS funded? Full Fact Check, Health/Health Spending, 6 July 2018. https://fullfact.org/health/how-nhs-funded (accessed 11 January 2024).

having worked in the UK for over 50 years. Mum was now retired and living on her pension. I knew she had a British passport and, like Dad, had worked all her life in this country and the latter years of her life for the council caring for older people. But despite that, I was concerned that if her papers were lost or something untoward happened in which her documentation could not be found, she could also suffer Albert's fate, along with thousands of other Caribbeans who had settled in Britain decades before.

But as I looked into Albert's dilemma, I was shocked when I found a law had been created to enable this to happen. It came in the guise of the National Health Service (Overseas Visitors) Charging (Amendment) Regulations 2017, which were introduced in October 2017. The regulations required that hospitals check patients' paperwork, including passports and proof of address, and charge upfront for their healthcare if they did not have documentary proof of eligibility unless the treatment was deemed to be urgent. It is up to the hospital to decide whether to require full payment upfront before starting a course of non-urgent treatment. So it may be possible for a person to start a course of treatment and then be invoiced for this afterward. Treatment that a clinician decides is urgent or immediately necessary must be provided regardless of whether advance payment has been received. All aspects of maternity care were considered to be "immediately necessary."

As of 23 October 2017, any organization providing NHS-funded secondary healthcare was required by law to secure full payment upfront for the total estimated cost of non-urgent treatment from an overseas visitor who is not exempt from charging. Where securing advance payment would prevent or delay the provision of immediately necessary or urgent treatment (including maternity services), the treatment must be provided regardless of whether the overseas visitor has paid upfront. When Albert's story broke, these regulations had been in place for less than a year. I went to see Mum to ensure her British passport and all her documents were in order. Mum provided me with evidence that all her paperwork was in place. I breathed a sigh of relief but was alert for any further legal change that could affect Mum and those like her.

On 14 March 2018, Jeremy Corbyn, the then Labour Leader, raised Albert's case in the House of Commons at Prime Minister's Questions. Theresa May, who was not familiar with Mr Thompson's case, refused to intervene and wrote in a letter to the Labour leader: "No urgent treatment should ever be withheld or delayed by the NHS regardless of ability or willingness to pay … The decision on whether his treatment is urgent or immediately necessary must rightly be made by the clinicians treating him."[6] Following Albert's case being raised within the media and in Parliament, the Prime Minister confirmed that Albert Thompson would receive NHS treatment and that treatment subsequently commenced.

Laura Stahnke of Praxis, a charity that provides practical, legal, and emotional support for migrants in crisis or at-risk, who were helping Thompson with his immigration problems, said,

> "We are delighted … Nevertheless, the fact that he had to go through an endless series of media interviews, having his case debated in Parliament, to access his right to health care is scandalous."[7]

In April 2018, the Government was forced to apologise for the trauma they had caused to so many people who had made Britain their home for decades. But this was about so much more than just a piece of legislation, because the Government had effectively placed the life of Albert in the hands of an administrative process, one in which a nurse was left to explain to a man, dealing with such a fearful diagnosis, that he was required to pay, within the confines of a hospital corridor. Theresa May had put a policy into place, with no understanding of not just those who would become victims of it but also those responsible for implementing it.

I thought back to how awful I felt that day when I saw that agency worker walk away, uncertain as to whether they would return to work. I recall how difficult it was to explain the process to them and how devastating it was to see them break down in tears. Theresa May had not factored in what difficult positions hospitals and other organizations would be faced with in dealing with administering the *hostile environment*.

Labour MP David Lammy sent an outraged letter to the Government signed by 140 cross-party MPs and, in April 2018, made the following speech in Parliament:

---

6. Gentleman, Amelia, "Theresa May promises to look into man's £54,000 NHS cancer bill," *Guardian*, 14 March 2018.
7. Gentlemen, Amelia, *Guardian*, 24 April 2018.

"…It is inhumane and cruel for so many of that Windrush Generation to have suffered so long in this condition…can she [the Secretary of State] tell the house how many have been detained as prisoners in their own country…how many have been denied health under the National Health Service, how many have been denied pensions, how many have lost their jobs. This is a day of national shame…"[8]

Although Albert's treatment had commenced, there was no telling what damage had been done, due to the delay in starting it. As I read further stories like Albert's, an uneasiness took hold, one I couldn't shake because I could not understand why, when it became clear that Caribbeans who had made Britain their home and had resided here for over 40 years were being caught up in this, and after it had been brought to the Government's attention nothing was done to remedy this.

Further suspicions were raised when in April 2018, Diane Abbott, the former Labour Shadow Home Secretary, stated that a critical legal change was made in the Immigration Act 2014. Previously, all longstanding Commonwealth residents were protected from enforced removal by a specific exemption in the 1999 Immigration and Asylum Act. It was this clause that was removed in the revised 2014 legislation.[9] The Home Office said the clause was not included in the 2014 Immigration Act because adequate protections were already in place for people initially granted temporary rights to remain in the UK and who have stayed for decades. The Labour Party, lawyers, and charities urged the Government to reinstate the clause to ensure all longstanding Commonwealth residents were protected from enforced removal, not just those like Mum, who have gained settled status.

Equally disturbing was a report in the *Guardian* that revealed that the issue of older Caribbean-born residents being wrongly classified as illegal immigrants was raised formally in 2016 by Caribbean foreign ministers and the then Foreign Secretary, Philip Hammond, during the biannual UK Caribbean Forum held that year in Freeport, the Bahamas. The High Commissioner to one affected

8. Demainyk, Graeme, "David Lammy Condemns Treatment of Windrush Generation as a 'National Day Of Shame,'" *Huffington Post*, 16 April 2018.
9. "Tory Leaders and Policies are to Blame for the Windrush Scandal," The Blog, Diane Abbott, 17 April 2018.

Caribbean country said officials alerted the Foreign Office to the problem at least half a dozen times from as early as 2013 onwards, to no avail.[10]

Lucy Moreton, head of the Immigration Service Union (ISU), that for Borders, Immigration and Customs staff, also flagged concerns at the time, stating that face-to-face interviews with the visa and immigration applicants vanished around 2014, which she believed had a bearing on what happened with the Windrush Generation. "You could talk to them," she said of the earlier system. "There's a commonality of experience that someone who has grown up here will have. You get a sense they're genuine. In 2014, discretion was removed. You ended up with a checklist approach."[11]

However, the erosion of rights for Commonwealth citizens came into play as early as 1988. Previously, all Commonwealth citizens' rights were protected to come and go as they wished. There was no timeline for this, a protection that was also extended to their wives (not husbands) and children who joined them. However, the Immigration Act 1988 removed that protection for any Commonwealth citizen, or others settled in the UK, to remain indefinitely after a two-year absence. It also removed the right of wives and children to join them.

Why were all these warning signs being ignored? Why was the Government so stubborn in failing to fix the problem for those Caribbeans and Commonwealth citizens caught up in the hostile environment trap? Did racism have a part to play in how the Windrush Generation was being treated? Some did not think so.

In 2018, in a blog titled Weaponising Victimhood,[12] when discussing victims caught up in the Windrush Scandal, Munira Mirza said:

"The Government's attempt to impose a hostile environment on illegal immigrants inadvertently caught a small group of older people of Caribbean heritage who had not needed papers when they first arrived in Britain."

Mirza went on to state,

---

10. Gentleman, Amelia, "Revealed: Depth of Home Office Failures on Windrush," *Guardian*, 18 July 2018.
11. Ibid.
12. Mirza, Munira (2018), "Weaponising Victimhood," *All In Britain*, 12 May 2018.

"Their experiences were deeply distressing and were the fault of officials working under a badly designed process; a process that could have been more sensitive to these historic groups, who might struggle to prove their status. But was this really about race…stories exist of foreign-born white people experiencing a similar level of Kafkaesque misery at the hands of the Home Office, and the top three countries for forced deportation are all white European: Romania, Albania, and Poland."

Mirza stated, "The real lesson is not one of racism; rather, it is that the immigration enforcement process needs to be improved."[13]

To Munira Mirza, the mere suggestion that racism could have played a part in how Caribbeans of the Windrush Generation were treated is unfathomable. But does she, or anyone, have the right to make that call? She accepts that Caribbean experiences were, in her words, deeply distressing, and acknowledges that officials involved could have been more sensitive to what she calls these historical groups. Mirza it seems fails to understand that there is a reaction for every action. Neither she nor anyone has the right to conclude that an individual does not have the right to perceive that action as racism. Mainly when that individual has, throughout their life, had to deal with racism within different aspects of their life. In writing this blog, Mirza attacked the very heart of the right for individuals to think for themselves and draw conclusions about how they perceive they are being treated.

What about the officials and the process, which Mirza calls severely designed? What if there were more sinister motives behind how Caribbeans were unwittingly ensnared? Author and historian Ibram X Kendi made the case that much of conventional thinking around racism misses the point. Arguing that it is power and policy, and not people, that keep racism firmly entrenched in society. During an online conversation sponsored by the Yale Alumni Association, Kendi confronted what makes a person "racist": "It describes what a person is being in any given moment, based on what they are saying or not saying, doing or not doing."[14] To eliminate racism, Kendi told the audience that people must understand where it comes from. Many people have taken

---

13. Ibid.
14. Belli, Brita, "Kendi: Racism is about power and policy, not people," 7 December 2020, *Yale News.* https://news.yale.edu/2020/12/07/kendi-racism-about-power-and-policy-not-people (accessed 21 August 2021).

for granted that "the cradle of racism" is ignorance and hate. If that's the case, he said, it would stand to reason that once people are better educated, racist policies would end. But what if, he argued, the perpetrators of racist policies already know what you are trying to teach them? What if they are instituting racist policies out of self-interest?[15]

I was fascinated by Kendi's thinking about racism when applying it to the hostile environment policy and its impact on the Caribbean community settled in Britain. What if Government had no intention of people like Albert falling foul of it, but once they realised this was happening they chose to allow it to continue to "kill two birds with one stone." What other explanation could there be for their failure to correct the problem after warnings were given, and cases such as Albert's became common knowledge?

Further credence is given to this premise, with the plot thickening when, on 17 April 2018, the *Guardian* reported that a Home Office ex-employee revealed that it had destroyed thousands of landing card slips recording Windrush immigrants' arrival dates in the UK. This despite staff warnings that the move would make it harder to check records of older Caribbean-born residents experiencing residency difficulties. The decision to do so occurred in 2010 because these slips provided details of an individual's date of entry but did not provide reliable evidence relating to ongoing residence in the UK or their immigration status.

This has been contested by two Home Office whistleblowers arguing that the landing cards had been a helpful resource. The whistleblower's account is supported by the Border Force, where its notes state that "an entry clearance officer may use information from a landing card in deciding on a visa application." Destroying landing cards allowed Home Office staff to tell those concerned that they had no record of arrival dates, which would lead to the denial of services and, at worst, deportation. In addition, former Home Office employees detail how the "hostile environment" changed the attitude of staff to the point where they enjoyed catching out Windrush individuals without evidence.[16]

The more I read, the angrier I got. Was I building myself into a paranoia, and was this mere conjecture on my part? As a lawyer, I knew I had to be objective and look at the facts, but they all pointed to the same conclusion. This

---

15. Ibid.
16. EU Law Analysis, "Windrush: Violating data protection law under the guise of protecting it," Matthew White, PhD candidate Sheffield Hallam University, 19 April 2018 (unpublished).

was a racist policy that was impacting my community in ways we could not have imagined. As the stories unfolded, I realised that never before had being a lawyer meant so much to me. I was running a busy legal team within a significant local authority, dealing with various aspects of law; my only client was departments across the council, which was my bread and butter, and I paid my bills. It was a job I enjoyed, had settled into, and was committed to. But I realised I had spent all my legal life practising law but had lost the reason I became a lawyer in the first place, which was to help give not just myself but others within my community a voice. As stories unfolded of the Windrush victims, coupled with my journey, which had been fraught with difficulties, as well as dealing with the emotional trauma of my past and ancestral history, I began to question my role as a lawyer at the heart of which it was required that I would not "unfairly discriminate" by allowing my personal views to affect my professional relationships and how I provide my services. Within that comes crucial terms such as acting honestly and with integrity. All these are prerequisites to being a lawyer and are second nature in how I have lived within my professional and personal life.

When what I describe as Windrushgate ("The Home Office Scandal") came to light, I had to take a hard look at how possible it would be for me to detach my personal views from those responsible for creating "the hostile environment" which was ruining so many people's lives, breaking them down to a point where they just wanted to give up. What made it even more difficult was that many affected people were from the Caribbean, with the most significant numbers coming from Jamaica. In 2018 it was revealed that up to 15,000 Jamaicans may have been affected by the scandal.[17] My profession is what I do; it is not "who I am," so how do I reconcile myself to an unjust law that is disproportionately affecting those from my community?

As well as familiarising myself with cases like Albert's, my lack of knowledge of Windrush and all it entailed concerned me. Immigration law is a highly specialised area, and I needed to understand it better. With that in mind, I tapped into the wonders of modern-day technology to watch an online committee hearing. This did not make for easy viewing, as it highlighted just how deep the scandal went.

---

17. "Commonwealth Migrants Arriving Before 1971, Year Ending 2017," Migration Observatory.

CHAPTER 11

Paulette and Anthony

I n June 2018, Virgin Airlines announced that it would no longer assist the Home Office in deporting people classed as illegal immigrants, following pressure from LGBT campaigners and rising unease over the wrongful removal of Windrush people to Caribbean countries. Virgin Airlines has provided seats on its commercial flights to detainees and security staff accompanying them for years. A charity in Jamaica that helps resettle deported people from the UK said detainees regularly arrived as passengers on Virgin flights. British Airways had also deported individuals to Jamaica. In May 2018, former Home Secretary Sajid Javid admitted that at least 63 Windrush Generation people had been wrongly removed to the Caribbean, despite having lived in the UK since before 1971 and consequently being eligible for British citizenship.[1]

Sam Bjorn, a spokesperson from Lesbians and Gays Support the Migrants, said: "Virgin's role in enforcing deportations has been devastating to people taken, against their will, to countries where they risk persecution or which they have very little connection to. Not only did the airline unflinchingly put people's lives in danger for many years, it also made their staff unwillingly complicit in the brutality of the UK's hostile environment policy."[2]

Reading about the decision of Virgin Airlines kicked me into touch with something I had been in denial of; it was like watching a movie and turning it off before the end because you knew there would not be a happy ending. I could not get to grips with or accept the fact that innocent people were actually being deported and sent back to a country they had left years before, having made their lives in Britain and being forcibly removed from their families and homes by mistake on multiple occasions. It was incomprehensible to me. But

---

1. Gentleman, Amelia, "Virgin Airlines says it will no longer help to deport immigrants," *Guardian*, 29 June 2018.
2. Ibid.

irrespective of burying my head in the sand, I had to face the cruel reality that it was happening, and in doing so, the wonders of technology took me to the cases of Paulette Wilson and Anthony Bryan, two case studies I will never forget.

In 2018, Parliament set up a Joint Committee on Human Rights (JCHR) to consider the detention of two children from the Windrush Generation, Anthony and Paulette. Article 5 of the European Convention on Human Rights (ECHR) only permits interference with the right to liberty in specific circumstances. Individuals should not be deprived of freedom without good reason and adequate safeguards. Anthony's and Paulette's cases were critical because it required that senior management and the Home Office be questioned before MPs who formed the committee.

On 16 May 2018, the committee took evidence from Anthony and Paulette, who the Home Office detained even though they had a legal right to be in the UK under the Immigration Act 1971. In evidence, Anthony and Paulette indicated that they would like to see their Home Office case files to discover how the Home Office had made decisions about their status and eventually detained them. These files were provided to the committee, who were then able to raise specific issues from those files in a further meeting, which took place on 6 June 2018, in which newly appointed Home Secretary, Sajid Javid, and Glynn Williams, Director General for Immigration Policy in the Home Office, attended to respond to questions posed by the joint committee, chaired by Harriet Harman.

Committee member Fiona Bruce confirmed that Anthony Bryan's case file showed that an application was first made in 2014, supplemented by a letter from his solicitors in May 2015, when they sent to the Home Office a large amount of information, confirming what Bryan had said in respect of his immigration status. He arrived in the UK aged about nine years old, around 1965, and had never been out of the country since. His solicitors supported this by providing his National Insurance (NI) number, which went back to 1975, which HMRC (the tax office) had now confirmed. The solicitors also provided information about his primary school, medical records, his Jamaican passport with the number, his child's birth certificates, and payslips, all culminating in a large amount of documentation being submitted. Over the years, the immigration department raised further inquiries, and evidence from friends was supplied of residence in the UK, from his partner, and from his primary school. However,

Anthony Bryan was detained in September 2016 despite providing all that information. Further information was supplied, but he was then detained again in November 2017 and nearly deported. Even in January 2018, the Home Office was still writing to his solicitors asking for another interview despite having all this information to hand. The committee also referred to a letter written by Bryan's son in August 2015.

> "I am writing this letter on behalf of Anthony Bryan, my father. Anthony has been in my life for as long as I can remember. My father has lived in this country for over 45 years; during this time, he has always maintained employment and taught me wrong from right. I am currently 31 years old, married, and have two lovely boys; I am currently employed as a bus operator for a Bus company, which has been established for over 60 years. Since leaving school, I have always maintained work. I have never been in trouble with the law and have a clean criminal record. This is all down to the way my parents raised me. Words can't express what my father has done; his relationship with my children is fantastic. I hope this letter will give you an insight into what my father is about. If you need to contact me for any reason, please feel free to do so."[3]

The committee also pointed out that when Bryan was asked at the point of deportation which airport in Jamaica he wanted to fly to, he replied, "I don't know any airports in Jamaica, I don't know Jamaica."[4]

The committee asked on what basis the Home Office immigration department concluded that the evidence submitted in Bryan's case was insufficient. Glynn Williams responded, stating that the initial application was made about a right to remain under human rights based on his long residency in the UK. Williams then went on to state that this was effectively the wrong application, but this was not pointed out to Bryan at the time. Based on that, the application was treated on its merits as one with respect to human rights on the basis of his long residence. As such, they believed that insufficient evidence had been provided to establish his continued residence over a 20-year period. Williams stressed to the committee that he was not seeking to say this was the

---

3. JCHR, Detention of Windrush Generation, HC 1034, Houses of Parliament.
4. Ibid.

right decision. He was seeking to explain the "thinking" and the "workings" of the Home Office on that point. The immigration office felt that, firstly, they had not been provided with evidence that he had entered the UK in 1965, and secondly, there was insufficient evidence over a 20-year period.

In Paulette Wilson's case, she came to the UK in 1968 at the age of ten, and information was supplied in her case as it was in Bryan's. In addition, a letter was provided by the Jamaican High Commission in March 2017, actually confirming that Ms Wilson entered the UK as a small child, approximately ten years old. She had a daughter, granddaughter, and a large family in the UK. The commission went on to confirm that she has no recollection of Jamaica. Ms Wilson also spent some time in a children's home. She had 35 years of NI and medical records, and her daughter and a childhood friend produced evidence of her residence in the UK. Despite all that, she was detained twice, in August 2017 and October 2017, because "There was no current evidence of lawful entry."

The response from Williams to the committee on Ms Wilson's case was that she first submitted her application in 2003, which brought her to the attention of the immigration office. The application was not decided; it was rejected because it wasn't on a particular form, and a fee may not have been paid. There was a gap until 2014, when the Home Office was going through an exercise via a company, Capita, trying to track down people who may have been in the country without leave and to trace those people and see who had departed and who of them were still in the country. And that's how Capita came into contact with Paulette. Her case was subsequently passed to the Home Office.

There followed a two-year interaction with Ms Wilson, when she was invited to submit evidence via the No Time Limit (NTL) process, in which Williams accepted Paulette provided various pieces of evidence over the two years. Unfortunately, because the evidence was not done on an NTL form and the fee was not paid, the Home Office did not take a holistic view of that evidence, which Williams admitted was a mistake, acknowledging that they should have engaged more pro-actively because Ms Wilson was left bewildered and was not in a position to respond to something that was a legalistic and bureaucratic requirement of the Home Office.

It was accepted that she was clearly vulnerable. The committee drew Williams's attention to a one-line letter she wrote, giving her daughter's phone number, in which she said, "Please help me; this is my home."[5]

The committee was concerned that in both cases, neither Bryan nor Wilson produced a shred of evidence that cast doubt on what they had said. Their stories were consistent and holistic, yet the Home Office equally and consistently challenged their applications rather than validated them.

The committee referred to extreme distress suffered by relatives, documented by Paulette's daughter, who remonstrated with the Home Office, stating, "This is my mum." And those remonstrations resulted in her being banned from attending the Home Office with her mother. Harriet Harman was extremely upset by this, making her position clear by saying: "I must say, when I saw what the daughter had done on behalf of her mother, it was all I could do not to stand up and cheer for this woman because she was doing what any daughter would do when the mother was being subjected to a terrible injustice." Harman read the note to Williams that had been made by the Home Office officer in respect of the ban against Paulette's daughter: "I advised her mother that her daughter would not be allowed into the building in future, the daughter started to swear, stating you are an effing B. You can P off, It's my mum!"

Harman was shocked at the lack of compassion on the part of the Home Office regarding the stress suffered by Paulette's daughter, telling Williams: "The Home Office response was they banned the daughter and locked the mother up."[6] All Williams could say, was it was a badly managed case.

In giving evidence at the inquiry in May 2018, Paulette's daughter informed the committee:

> "When it came to my mum, I was furious and I was trying to say to them, 'Listen, you're doing the wrong thing. She was here before the law kicked in. It did not kick in until 1973. My mum has been here since 1968.' A guy swore at me. I swore back at him. I asked him 'Can you prove to me that you are English right now? Prove it. Take something out of your pocket to prove you are British. How do I know you're British and not from a different country?' He swore at me, and then I was banned from the Home

---

5. Ibid.
6. Ibid.

Office. They banned me from there because they said that I was causing a bit of a disturbance when I was going there because I was trying to fight for my mum."[7]

Paulette also provided evidence of what happened when she was released from detention:

"The day I was released, they put me outside the airport. The man who let me out said, 'A cab is going to pick you up and take you to the station.' I was outside the airport. I was in tears, crying, because the planes were taking off over my head. I had to stand and squeeze my head. I was praying for this taxi man to come and pick me up. They shoved me out. No-one stayed with me. I waited for the cab. The cab man came. He said, 'Are you Paulette Wilson?' I said, 'Yes.' He put me in the cab and took me to the station. They gave me a travel warrant from the station from here back to Wolverhampton, and that was it. I was on the Underground. Then I got to Euston and was put on the fastest train back to Wolverhampton. They have not said anything to me ever since."

As I listened to Paulette's evidence being read, I was filled with rage; I thought back to how I checked through Mum's papers to make sure they were all in order, and how my siblings and I breathed a sigh of relief on finding that they were. But as the only lawyer in the family, I knew if anything did happen, it would have been down to me to sort it out. When Dad died, I was left to deal with his probate, complete all the documents, and attend the probate office. But even though I was legally trained, it was one of the hardest things I had to do. Because you have lost someone that has been in your life all your life, and to those dealing with the administration of his passing, he was just a name, but to me, he was my Dad. Thinking about what Paulette's daughter had to go through in watching the horror story of the events unfold, I knew precisely why she acted the way she did and was glad that Harriet Harman understood that. If I had been in her shoes, I would have done my best to keep a clear head for Mum, but I would likely have been emotional and angry enough, not

---

7. Ibid.

only just to have been banned, but I probably would have come close to being arrested, in seeing mum being treated in this way.

This brought home to me the importance of your voice being heard and the devastating effect when that right is taken away. Paulette's daughter had every right to defend her mother, but in the eyes of the establishment, she had no power, no rights. Access to justice is a right that every citizen should expect, but for Paulette and her daughter and all the Windrush victims it fell silent. The scariest part was the lack of empathy of ordinary men and women working for the Home Office who were dealing with Paulette, Anthony and everyone like them. There was blind obedience in following these unfair practices; where was their humanity? The trauma of watching that hearing has remained with me and will do so for the rest of my life. But I had to be extremely careful in how I dealt with the bitterness and anger I felt.

Maya Angelou says, "Bitterness is like cancer; it eats upon the host." But goes on to say,

> "Anger is healthy, anger is like fire it burns out all the trash and all the stuff and I think it's wise to show it. To be opposed to injustice, at all times, for anybody, I think that's wise … It's much healthier, and fortunately, it's crea- tive, and that creative thing has a productive result."[8]

I took Maya's words and ran with them, as she gave me the empowerment not to be frightened by the anger I felt because that anger would help me to channel my skills and abilities as a lawyer into finding a way to help people like Paulette, her daughter, and Anthony.

The joint committee found that it was unacceptable that Home Office offi- cials overlooked the rights of a whole category of people with a legal right to be in the country. The consequent failure to make sure that policy accounted for them had severe consequences for the individuals concerned. They found evidence that the fact that there was no power to detain Anthony and Paulette was blithely ignored, which the committee considered hugely problematic. They thought that the Home Office's required standards of proof from members of the Windrush Generation went well beyond those required, even by its guidance;

---

8. Maya Angelou interview, Afternoon Plus, with Mavis Nicholson, Thames TV, 1984.

moreover, they were impossible for victims or anyone else to meet. The Home Office's decision determining they had reasons to detain Anthony and Paulette was simply unlawful. It did not accept the Home Office's explanation that the deficiencies in the handling of these cases were a result of "a series of mistakes over some time." Both cases had been repeatedly assessed, and different people within the Home Office took a series of decisions over a long period. Given that numerous officials handled these case files it is not plausible that the same mistakes could have been made repeatedly. Rather the pattern of errors pointed to the greater likelihood of a lack of both an appropriate system of case management, and of oversight by senior officers of compliance with such a system to minimise the possibility of such mistakes being made. Moreover, no disciplinary action, remedial action, or any fundamental review of procedures was taken by the Home Office as one would expect from an organization which has encountered such serious errors.

The committee was told there was a process for "quality assurance," but they do not have supporting details. The committee determined that if failings were the result of staff "mistakes" and poor decisions, then staff should be identified, disciplined, and retrained, as appropriate. However, it went further than that, as successive poor decisions and successive gross errors of judgement indicated a problem with the system itself, which, therefore, required more fundamental changes to policy, culture, and training.[9]

On 5 December 2018, the National Audit Office (NAO) published a report entitled "Handling of the Windrush Situation," which found that the Home Office failed in its duty "to be proactive in identifying people affected." It criticised the Home Office for poor-quality data that wrongly classified people as illegal immigrants, the risky use of deportation targets, poor value for money offered by hostile environment policies, and failure to respond to numerous warnings that the policies would hurt people living in the UK legally.[10]

Paulette's and Anthony's stories were just two of many. I knew I had to do something; the question was, *what?*

---

9. JCHR, Detention of Windrush Generation, HC 1034, Houses of Parliament.
10. "Handling of the Windrush Situation," National Audit Office, 5 December 2018. https://www. nao.org.uk/reports/handling-of-the-windrush-situation/ (accessed 11 January 2024).

CHAPTER 12

Time to Leave Hackney and Go It Alone

We were approaching the Autumn of 2018 and Hackney was undergoing a restructuring within the legal team, which gave me the opportunity for the more senior role of Head of Litigation (of the court legal team). As with most restructures, my colleagues and I were uneasy as we deliberated on what lay ahead. I had been working in Hackney for 12 years and had made some great friends and a secure niche within an organization, in which I was respected. The new role would not only have increased my wage; it would have taken me on a road onto which I would move from a senior lawyer to the higher echelons of executive legal management. From there, the only way would have been to continue to excel; there was no telling how far I could go.

But I didn't apply for the role because something was happening within me. My brush with Windrush had had a profound effect on me, and reading about Albert, Paulette, and Anthony, all my research, as well as sitting in the library just a few months before, trying to help my colleague caught up in the scandal, made me take a long hard look at myself. I realised at that point that it wasn't just about that job; it was me and everything that I was doing. I had worked so hard to get to this juncture in my life it was only logical that the step would be upwards. But that wasn't important anymore; it was not enough. The truth is, you can lie to everyone else, but you can never lie to yourself; something had awakened in me that told me I was not fulfilled.

I had a heart-to-heart with my husband, Everton, and told him how I was feeling. As I opened up, it became clear that it was time to move on and leave Hackney. However, the dilemma I faced was that I did not want to slot myself back into another prosecution role in another borough. I had gained a lot of experience in several areas, not just criminal so on paper would have had no problem finding another job. But that's not what I wanted; I needed a clean break. My colleagues were shocked to discover I had handed in my letter of resignation, and my manager called me into her office and did her best to persuade me to stay. "If you could just hold on for a year, I can guarantee that you can apply for redundancy and get a big payout."

Maybe it was the sceptic in me, but I had been in local government long enough to know that nothing was guaranteed, and no-one knew where we would be in a year. Also, even though some of my colleagues were securing great redundancy packages, my role was not included in the restructuring programme. Therefore, the options open to me were staying in my current role, applying for a more senior position, holding on for a year to see if I would be paid off, or leaving. As it had never been about money, the choice was easy; I thanked my manager but stood by my decision to walk away.

"Where are you going?" my colleagues asked, assuming I had been offered another job. But there was no new job. As with Kent, I left Hackney, in late December 2018, jobless. It was a scary time, but we had enough savings for me to be off work for three to four months. A redundancy package would have given me the financial security to be out of work for more time, but it was not to be.

"Lard Jesus, how yu going to manage," Mum asked as I sat on her bed and told her my decision. Dad had died five years before, and as a family we were strong but missing him. My sister was nervous, but they trusted my decision and knew my mind was made up. I knew I could always rely on my family if we fell into financial difficulty.

January 2019 was a new start. As I watched the fireworks explode from my bedroom window, I hugged my husband and cuddled the cat, excited and slightly apprehensive about what was in store. The following three months of my life were a journey of self-discovery. I began writing my first non-fiction book with the working title *Black People Must Have Done Something Bad*. I described it as a gut-wrenching, truth-seeking missile that dared to ask the question: "Are black people to blame for hiding their inadequacies behind the smokescreen of racism?" I aimed to provide the reader with an adrenaline boost by introducing readers to a generation brought up on *Rice and Peas and Fish and Chips* (the eventual title of the book). Scuppered by Thatcherism, let down by New Labour and thrown into poverty by austerity, portraying all the trimmings of a political thriller, illustrating how immigration had been used throughout the decades as the catalyst in securing votes to the detriment of the immigrant population.

I wanted to get back into my community because it wasn't until I left Hackney that I realised how detached I'd become from the black community I'd grown up in. The danger of wanting to be the best you can be within any chosen profession is that you risk forgetting what's important. The irony was not lost on me how, years before, I had decided to leave Kent to return to a more diverse community, which was so important to me then. Still, despite my best intentions, I had fallen away from that community to pursue my career in law.

Although I moved from Tottenham to Walthamstow in 2007, I still had strong connections in Tottenham through people and local organizations that I knew. I had been incredibly unsettled by the increasing violence within the black community, mainly when it came to young black people, and I needed to know if racism was the key, the catalyst, or if there was more. Were black people to blame? Had we let these young people down by not fighting hard enough to be heard—to help those young people from our community who were either in gangs, jobless, or excluded from the education system?

I attended community meetings and conferences, sat on panels discussing how to tackle the issues of knife crime and read articles and books on British history, the history of the British Empire, and how it impacted communities worldwide. I watched endless archive footage, which included several online lectures, in my search for answers to how the black community got to this point. I loved history, talking about it from an informed position, making it enjoyable, and bringing it alive. It enabled me to link our history with the Windrush Generation and tie in with the scandal and all it entailed.

I had found my purpose; it was to educate people, black and white, young and old, on the importance of how we are all part of history in the making. When it comes to social justice it does not just dictate our past but can also help us to understand our future. I dreamed of giving lectures in schools and universities and becoming an expert on TV panels alongside famous historical lecturers. It took me just three months to complete my book; I was obsessed starting at 5 am and working until eight at night; it was a living collage of racism in words.

I subscribed to several successful non-fiction writers' forums, highlighting vital pointers, such as "Why is this topic important?", "Why does it stand out?", "What is the bigger picture?" I found out how to write a book proposal that would pop and grab a literary agent's attention. I spent hours watching and making notes. However, the forums also suggested that it's always best to get an independent opinion from an experienced editor before submitting a book. I was warned that there are several charlatans/con artists who would happily take the money of desperate authors, all hoping for that bestseller. With that in mind, I used my research skills to seek out a reputable writers' agency, which provided me with references from various editors that they employed, with credentials to support their expertise in this area. Therefore, I used £980 of my now dwindling savings to provide me with a review of my 90,000-word manuscript.

Ten days later, a 17 page report was received; the editor was extremely generous in her opening, making it clear that my book had been "Intelligently written and extensively researched, relying upon expert opinion, articles, TV documentaries, and eyewitness accounts. It is written objectively and authoritatively, blending historical facts and contemporary statistics with elements from the author's life. This adds a personal touch, with poignant anecdotes from her childhood and adulthood."

The editor unpicked every aspect of each chapter, highlighting the highs, the lows, the ups and the downs. I read each page encouraged that my endeavours of the past three months had not been in vain, and it was nice to know all my research had been acknowledged by a professional, as she went on to state:

> "The author makes excellent use of chapter headings in the book. This skill should not be undervalued or under-appreciated as many authors don't realise the importance of having attention-grabbing, intriguing or enticing chapter headings. The author uses source materials, often quite disturbing and upsetting information, to support her arguments."

However, when I got to the page on marketability, my heart dropped, with the editor telling me how there were currently over 30,000 books about racism on Amazon.com, over 70,000 books about Black History, and over 20,000 for Black British History, therefore for my book to stand out, I needed an "angle" a unique selling point. She stated:

"As the book currently stands, I think it will be tricky to find a mainstream publisher. This bears no reflection on the quality of the book or the writing. Many traditional publishers are currently struggling financially, so they are looking for mass-market best sellers or niche genre books to make them money. They are less interested in whether the author is a great writer, an authority in their field, or whether the topic is fascinating. Their primary interests are whether this book is sellable and how easily it will sell."

However, my most significant disadvantage was that I was unknown and did not have a social media following. Although the editor provided me with various tips on how to start building on this, and I had purchased books on this topic, I had to accept that it would be an uphill struggle. Also, time and cost were against me. I had been out of work for three months, and unexpected bills and increased costs had placed me and my husband in a difficult position.

After a heavy conversation with my husband, I decided to sign up with some legal agencies to see if I could find prosecution work within a local authority. Still, at the same time, I would continue to work on building my profile and establishing the unique selling point of my book that would make it stand out. I also continued to work with the community, which included writing a couple of short scripts for a black theatre company that held drama classes for young people in Tottenham; the first was a piece on knife crime, and the other a celebration of black inventors. Seeing my scripts come alive through the voices of the talented young actors was beautiful. The best part of this was it came so naturally to me; it was fantastic to at last be giving something back to my community.

Two weeks later, an agency contacted me and told me about a senior lawyer prosecution post within Waltham Forest Council, which was just 20 minutes away. I agreed for my CV to be sent over and was immediately given an interview. On arrival at my local town hall, I met a fantastic woman who was the head of the litigation team and dealt with all the court cases. We spoke for over two hours, and before I arrived home I was contacted by the agency, confirming they would like to offer me the job. Although it was a relief that I would be earning a steady income again, I wished I had more time to continue my journey of self-discovery with no distractions.

April 2019 was significant for two reasons. The first was when I started my new job as a senior lawyer for Waltham Forest, and the second was the Windrush Compensation Scheme (WCS). The Government created the scheme to provide financial support to individuals who incurred losses due to the difficulties of proving their immigration status in the UK. Although relieved to be back on a wage, I was also disappointed that my new role would hinder my ability to help the Windrush victims with their compensation claims.

At its launch, Diane Abbott, the then Shadow Home Secretary, described the scheme as "shoddy, unfair, and unjust."[1] With a primary application form consisting of 44 pages with several guidance notes. Despite the complexities of the application process, no legal help was available to those applying for compensation other than civil legal advice (CLA), a national telephone service and a website that provided free legal advice on civil matters. However, the issues raised regarding Windrush cases would be complex, requiring detailed support from a lawyer with relevant expertise, which the telephone and website would be unable to provide.

Although former Home Secretary Amber Rudd announced the decision to create the scheme in April 2018, an elongated consultation process delayed its launch. Had it been in place when I left Hackney, I could have offered my services voluntarily to Citizens' Advice, law centres, or other organizations in need of legal assistance. I could have helped victims complete applications, gather evidence, and draft letters. But now, my new job would have made that problematic because, as a senior lawyer in a new post, running a busy team, I needed to prioritise that. Although four months was a relatively short period to be out of work, it would still take me time to acclimatise myself back into a nine-to-five life.

But I was a different person to the Pauline who had left Hackney just a few months before. My research had made me highly conscious of the importance of history alongside the inequalities that existed around me, and even though I knew that my legal work would take up a lot of my time, I was adamant that I would not forsake the real me ever again. I would find a way to continue my journey of self-discovery. I prayed that this would allow me to continue my work with those impacted by the Windrush Scandal.

---

1. Windrush Compensation Scheme, Volume 658, 9 April 2019, *Hansard*, UK Parliament.

PART II
FINDING MY VOICE

CHAPTER 13

Entering the World of Social Justice

I had been working in Waltham Forest for nearly a year. It had been a baptism by fire, as I had to hit the ground running. There was a lot of work, and I needed to make my mark as soon as possible to gain the trust of the lawyers and legal officers I managed. We also represented various client departments within the organization. My Head of Law and I got on immediately. She worked incredibly hard and was the most supportive manager I had ever had. It also helped that I worked so close to home, which took away a lot of stress with travelling and expenses, and all my colleagues were pleasant and professional. However, as with Hackney, I was acutely aware of the fact that the hierarchy of senior positions across the council consisted mainly of white males.

My work ethos had not changed since leaving Hackney; I was still the first one in and one of the last out. But my three months off had given me a thirst for knowledge, historical and current. I loved politics, reading relevant articles of the day, subscribing to quality newspapers, as well as BBC History Extra, which had some fantastic podcasts and articles. However, one of the most significant changes for me was my growing interest in the inequalities that existed within the legal profession. Every week, I received the *Law Society Gazette*, a British weekly legal magazine for solicitors in England and Wales published by the Law Society, which is provided to all solicitors with a practising certificate and other interested parties. The *Gazette* offers up-to-the-minute national and international news, opinion, features, in-depth articles, plus an appointments section.

On 23 March 2020, I read an article about the clash between the judiciary and the former Attorney-General, Suella Braverman, on the supremacy of Parliament within the British constitution. Usually, I would read the article and put it to one side. Still, in this case, I felt that it was vital that I made my thoughts known, which I did by writing to the *Gazette* opinion page in a piece entitled "Forcing Change on a Reluctant Judiciary."[1] I highlighted how, on the one hand, judges were fighting for their right to uphold the principles of equality under the law, a crucial element of which is the need for independent judges. On the other hand, they were reluctant to embrace diversity within their ranks, with just one per cent black judges. A few weeks later, my piece was printed on the opinion page and placed on the website.

On 18 May 2020, the *Gazette* published another of my pieces on the opinion page, "Nothing Changes if Nothing Changes."[2] Considering a study that revealed that ethnic minorities have to send in 60% more CVs than their white counterparts, even when they have the same qualifications. This evidence of labour market discrimination had barely changed in 50 years. Although I agreed that a candidate should get a job based on their ability rather than their ethnicity, I stressed that this system can only work if all candidates start from a level playing field.

It was satisfying having my thoughts published, and it also took me from just reading from the sidelines to proactively engaging. I had no idea that just a week later, I would be faced with the true evils of what racism and inequality could bring.

On 25 May 2020, I, along with millions, watched in horror as in the USA the knee of a police officer was pressed into the neck of George Floyd for 18 minutes and 46 seconds, with such ferocity that it ended his life. The murder, shared on video through social media before being televised, sent shock waves throughout the world, resulting in protests across the globe in the fight against inequality and racism. Although horrendous, the murder and disproportionate treatment of young black men at the hands of the police was all too familiar to the black community in the US and UK.

Reports revealed that the US police kill one thousand people, disproportionately black, every year and that racial disparities in policing mirrored entrenched racial disparities in almost all aspects of life, namely health, housing, education, employment, rates of arrest, and criminal convictions. The Covid-19 pandemic has magnified these disparities, with black people and people of colour disproportionately affected.[3]

---

1. Campbell, Pauline (2020), *Law Society Gazette*, March 23.
2. Campbell, Pauline (2020), *Law Society Gazette*, May 18.
3. "UN Rights Body Should Create International Inquiry into Systematic Racism and Police Violence in the US": UN Human Rights Urgent Debate, 18 June 2020, Human Rights Watch. https://www.hrw.org/news/2020/06/18/un-rights-body-should-create-international-inquiry-systemic-racism-and-police (accessed 18 January 2022).

In Britain, in 2020, young black men were stopped and searched by police more than 20,000 times during the coronavirus lockdown. More than 80% of the 21,950 searches between March and May 2020 resulted in no further action, according to analysis by the office of the Home Affairs Select Committee chair, Yvette Cooper. The figures equate to 30% of all young black males in London, though some individuals may have been searched more than once. The Metropolitan Police increased its use of stop and search during the lockdown compared to the year before. The force carried out 43,000 stops in May 2020, compared to 21,000 a year earlier, and 30,608 in April 2020, up from 20,981.[4]

But only one in five stops led to an arrest, fine, or caution, prompting renewed concerns that police are using the power indiscriminately. Maurice McLeod, the chief executive of Race On the Agenda (ROTA), said:

> "The increased proportion of stops that result in no action suggests that stops are being carried out based on officers' pre-existing biases rather than on genuine suspicion of criminality."[5]

However, despite increased stops and searches and the pandemic taking hold, protests continued to spill out on the streets in response to George Floyd's murder. In June 2020, I, along with the rest of the country, with the world looking on, watched as the statue of slave trader Edward Colston was torn down during an anti-racism protest in Bristol by angry protestors, one of which was seen with his knee on the figure's neck, reminiscent of the video of George Floyd. The statue was defaced and daubed with paint before being thrown into Bristol harbour. Several statues and memorials were the subject of similar protests and petitions in 2020 across the UK, including that of Winston Churchill in Parliament Square, which had graffiti sprayed on it over two successive days.

On 12 February 2021, I listened with interest as Priti Patel MP, then Home Secretary, told Nick Ferrari on LBC in respect of the Black Lives Matter movement:

---

4. Grierson, Jamie (Home Affairs Correspondent), "Met carried out 22,000 searches on young black men during lockdown," *Guardian*, 8 July 2020.
5. Beckford, Martin, "Stop-and-search use in London rose 40% in lockdown, figures show," *Guardian*, 25 August 2020.

"Last summer was quite a moment for all the protests that we saw taking place …we saw policing coming under a great deal of pressure through some of the protests …Those protests were dreadful …There are other ways; last summer was not the right way at all …we also saw statues being brought down …There are other ways in which these discussions can take place, and I didn't support that attempt to re-write history; I felt that was wrong."[6]

It was impossible not to be affected by what was happening around me. The question was, "What do I do about it?" For the first time, black people were not standing alone; others were standing alongside us in the fight against racism. The world around me was changing, and I was determined to be instrumental in that. This helped me further identify my purpose, which could no longer just consist of being a lawyer.

Therefore, in 2020, I joined the council's Race Equality Network (REN), and within months became the co-chair. The decision to be at the helm of REN was not a difficult one because I knew how complex my journey had been, and therefore I was invested in being proactive in pushing for change. Although much of my focus was on equality and diversity strategies, my key message was to speak truth to power honestly, where I provided a voice for the realities of non-white staff's experience. This I brought to life through using my advocacy skills which led to tangible change concerning the ethnicity pay gap strategy, recruitment approaches, and organization-wide equalities.

One of my most important initiatives was the creation of the Safe Space Clinic (SSC), a pilot scheme to work with staff experiencing inequality. I worked alongside managers to provide staff with a voice to air their concerns, identify what management could do differently, and improve conditions in the workplace. I thought back to all the times I had to stay silent when I was suffering and felt so much anger and frustration about my treatment, wishing there was someone there to give me a voice. I was passionate about leading difficult conversations to engender change and helping staff say what needed to be told rather than bottle it up. For me, REN was about so much more than being limited to the confines of Waltham Forest.

---

6. "I wouldn't take the knee in support of Black Lives Matter," LBC, 12 February 2021.

CHAPTER 14

The Importance of Sharing My Story

It was impossible not to be affected by what was happening around me because, following George Floyd's death (*Chapter 13*), it seemed we had reached a crossroads, with the world erupting into action. I dared to dream that maybe things would be different this time. That we could actually make positive, progressive steps toward real change. I was working hard within the REN, and our membership was growing. Although we were gaining strength, some members still felt that it was unlikely that anything would change.

At one of our meetings, a black colleague said that thinking we could level the playing field bordered on insanity. The statement shocked me because it showed hopelessness; I was not prepared to buy into it. However, I was mindful of the fact that even though several white people had spoken up about issues that affected the black and brown community, most within the workplace were content to be silent, only considering the problems of racial inequality from the sidelines. However, I noticed for the first time that some white officers, previously happy to maintain the status quo, were openly standing alongside us in the fight against racism. Some even went as far as writing emails to senior management about the need for equality within the workplace.

I knew it was up to me to take a leap of faith, find my voice, and invest proactively in pushing for change. My key message was to honestly speak truth to power, where I provided a voice for the realities of non-white staff's experience by openly talking about what I had been subjected to. About how that made me feel.

It wasn't easy at first. I was apprehensive about letting my guard down; the wall that I had built around me for protection had been in place for so long that I was nervous about breaking it down. My silence had provided me with a safety net, kept me under the radar, which is a comfortable place to be. I was concerned that sharing my story would leave me open to reprisals, which could affect my prospects as a senior lawyer within Waltham Forest. But the biggest hurdle within my decision was the fear of what sharing my experiences would do to me emotionally because I would effectively be opening old wounds that I knew had never really been given a chance to heal. What would that do to me?

Holocaust survivor and Nobel Prize winner Elie Wiesel said:

> "Of course, we could try to forget the past. Why not? Is it not natural for a human being to repress what causes him pain, what causes him shame? Like the body, memory protects its wounds."[1]

Black student and mentee of Elie Weisel, Sonari Glinton, recalled Weisel's words of wisdom when Glinton found the need to apologise for finding it hard not being able to "get past" the racism that existed around him, wishing he could "get beyond it." Weisel told him:

> "Memory wasn't just for Holocaust survivors. The people who ask us to forget are not our friends. Memory not only honours those we lost but also gives us strength. In those office hours, he gave me a shield, practical words, and thoughts that would help me—a gay, Nigerian, Catholic journalist. He gave me tools that would aid me in an often-hostile world. Over the years, I have found myself quoting Professor Wiesel to white people who want me to 'get over race.' That's old. It was a hundred years ago. But Professor Wiesel had been emphatic: 'Nothing good comes of forgetting; remember, so that my past doesn't become your future.'"[2]

The unique words of Weisel to his mentee Sonari helped me to put my reservations to one side because I had to speak out, not from a place of confrontation, accusation, or attaching guilt to white colleagues, but from a level in which I hoped to provide them with a fundamental understanding of what it meant to live in this skin. To exist within a working environment in which inequalities in respect of the ethnicity pay gaps and recruitment, among others, continued to exist.

---

1. Elie Wiesel, Nobel Lecture, 11 December 1986.
2. Glinton, Sonari, "Forgetting Isn't Healing: Lessons From Elie Wiesel," *Code Switch*, 14 July 2016. https://www.npr.org/sections/codeswitch/2016/07/14/484558040/forgetting-isnt-healing-lessons-from-elie-wiesel (accessed 19 January 2024).

Creating the SSC was an essential part of that journey. It was a pilot scheme to work with staff experiencing inequality. I worked alongside senior managers, which included directors and heads of service to provide staff with a voice to air their concerns, identify what management could do differently, and improve conditions in the workplace. I thought back to all the times I had to stay silent when I was suffering so much anger and frustration at my treatment wishing there was someone there to give me a voice at that time. I was passionate about leading difficult conversations to drive for change and help staff say what needed saying rather than bottling it up, which had a direct effect on their mental well-being.

Dealing with these difficult issues helped me to address a topic that, for my generation, was considered taboo. The stigma around mental health in the black community has long been an issue that has prevented those who need help from seeking it. Talking to mental health staff and sharing painful memories provided me with a release, which I had not expected. I had no idea of the profound effect of the emotional toll that my experiences had had on me until I began speaking openly about them.

Black British Voices (BBV) research found that nearly 70 per cent of those questioned said they or members of their family had battled with mental health issues.[3] One person who was interviewed said: "When we grew up, we never used to see our parents complain. They'll just take it on the chin, like slavery. So I feel like it's just embedded in us."[4] As I ventured further down the rabbit hole of what I could only describe as my "awakening," it became clear how people's mental health is impacted by racism. The BBV study found that mental health problems are likely to occur among people who are struggling financially and living in poverty, and when racism is added to these other societal factors, such as poor housing or school exclusions, it can have a major impact on mental health.[5]

Financial inequality, caused by lack of opportunity to progress into more senior and well-paid positions, continues to be a serious issue for black employees, which can only exacerbate mental health issues within the workplace, with the BBV report revealing that the UK's ethnicity pay gap has persisted over the

3. Black British Voices: i-Cubed, *The Voice*, University of Cambridge, October 2023.
4. Ibid.
5. Ibid.

past decade, when factors like occupation, qualifications, geography, age, and sex are taken into account. Among UK-born workers, black employees had the biggest pay gap, earning 5.6 per cent less than white employees. Non-UK-born black employees registered the highest pay gap in 2022, earning 12 per cent less than UK-born white workers, according to the statistics produced by the ONS.[6]

These statistics were a rude awakening for me as a lawyer. Figures released show that black, Asian, and minority ethnic solicitors earn less overall and occupy fewer senior positions. This contributes to an ethnicity pay gap of 25% when comparing hourly pay, which equates to a difference of £9.12 an hour. Comparing average annual salaries for full-time solicitors adds to a difference of more than £20,000 per year.[7] In addition to these figures, it was hard to take on board that a trainee solicitor employed in one of the large, lucrative, "Magic Circle" law firms would enter the profession on a wage that exceeded that of my own as a senior lawyer with 20 years' experience. This salary would double on qualification to up to £125,000.

I realised that familiarising myself with these figures was not enough; it was equally important to highlight the lack of social mobility within the legal world, which was detrimental to those within the profession. Therefore, I wrote an article for the *New Law Journal* entitled "Time to Pick Up the Pace on Social Mobility?"[8] It was the first piece I had written for that journal, and I was pleased when it was published. However, the article also showed me that my platform for using my voice could be broadened to reach a wider audience.

6. "Ethnicity pay gaps UK: 2021 to 2022," ONS, 29 November 2023. https://www.ons.gov.uk/employmentandlabourmarket/peopleinwork/earningsandworkinghours/articles/ethnicitypaygapsingreatbritain/2012to2022 (accessed 19 January 2023). Garcia, Carmen Aguilar, Duncan, Pamela, "'Absolutely shameful' UK ethnicity pay gap persists, figures show," *Guardian*, 29 November 2023. https://www.theguardian.com/world/2023/nov/29/absolutely-shameful-uk-ethnicity-pay-gap-persists-figures-show (accessed 19 January 2023).
7. "Ethnicity Pay Gap: What 'You Need to Know," *Law Society Gazette*, 22 November 2023. https://www.lawsociety.org.uk/topics/ethnic-minority-lawyers/ethnicity-pay-gap-do-we-really-need-it (accessed 19 January 2024).
8. Campbell, Pauline (2023), *New Law Journal*, May 5.

CHAPTER 15

Behind the Race Disparity Report

O n 8 June 2020, then Prime Minister Boris Johnson addressed the nation saying:

> "We cannot ignore the depths of emotion that has been triggered by the spectacle of a black man losing his life at the hands of the police. In this country and around the world, his dying words 'I can't breathe' have awakened an anger and widespread incontrovertible and undeniable feeling of injustice. A feeling that people from black and minority ethnic groups do face discrimination in education, in employment, and in the application of the criminal law. And we who lead and govern can't ignore those feelings because, in too many cases, I'm afraid they would be founded on a cold reality."[1]

Within weeks of Johnson's address, the UK Government set up the Commission on Race and Ethnic Disparity, to which Johnson gave a brief on investigating race and ethnic disparities in the UK. He argued that the UK needed to consider important questions about race relations and disparities. That a thorough examination of why so many disparities persist was needed to work out how to eliminate or mitigate them.

On the one hand, I was pleased that the Government had acknowledged that racial disparities were prevalent in UK society, but on the other hand, I felt an overwhelming sense of frustration that to address this they felt the need to commission *yet another* report despite the plethora of recommendations already in existence on this topic, going back over 40 years.

---

1. Boris Johnson's words on Black Lives Matter, 10 Downing Street, 8 June 2020. https://www. youtube.com/watch?v=6u6nPRC8gAo

At the time, former Interim Director of the Runnymede Trust, Dr Zubaida Haque, stated:

> "Here we have a Prime Minister, who is commissioning yet another review into racial inequalities, in the backdrop of so many reviews, we can barely count them, but hundreds of recommendations, which are not only telling us what the racial inequalities are but they're also giving us a plan of action, but this Government has clearly ignored that."[2]

This was a tough time for me, having the lived experience of being a teenager during the 1981 summer riots and reading the Scarman Report following those riots (*Chapter 7*), which provided a blueprint for what was required in order to create a more level playing field. As well as seeing the pain and tribulations suffered by Stephen Lawrence's parents and family following his racist murder, which eventually led to the McPherson Report.[3] That report found the police to be institutionally racist, making 70 recommendations, which included measures to not just transform the attitude of the police towards race relations and improve accountability but also to get the Civil Service, NHS, judiciary, and other public bodies to respond to change.

Having familiarised myself with all these and other reports, it was impossible not to feel deflated and despondent. But what alternative did I have other than to get on board and actively ensure I was engaged with the process? Irrespective of my misgivings, the worst thing I could do was not allow my voice to be heard. I had been silent for so long and had wasted so many years not believing it was important. In any event, the report would go ahead, regardless of whether I liked it or not.

I thought back to my days as a trainee solicitor and how, when I was at my lowest, I tapped into the wisdom and experience of those who came before me. Those involved in the Civil Rights Movement, my own parents, and others like them, who were welcomed to British shores with a colour bar and greeted with signs, "No Blacks, No Dogs, No Irish," long before any reports or recommendations were made in respect of racial injustices. I owed it to them to keep

---

2. "Labour demands action not reviews—after Boris Johnson announces racial inequality commission," Channel 4 News, 15 June 2020. https://www.youtube.com/watch?v=-r4_sJn_56s
3. "The Stephen Lawrence Inquiry: Report of an Inquiry by Sir William MacPherson," February 1999.

going and to not give up. I held out that maybe, just maybe, things would be different this time.

In June 2020, Munira Mirza, then head of the No. 10 Policy Unit, was the person Boris Johnson chose to lead the Commission on Race and Ethnic Disparity. To me, this was an instant red flag due to what seemed to be her staunch opposition to the idea that racism could be factored into why inequalities existed, what Mirza had described as a "culture of grievance."[4] Some critics claimed that with Mirza at the helm, the commission would be "dead on arrival."[5] Let me explain why such an opinion might exist and may have validity.

In October 2017, the Government published its Race Disparity Audit,[6] ordered by former Prime Minister Theresa May to tackle what she called the "burning injustices arising from people's race and background." The audit examined how people of different backgrounds are treated across areas including health, education, employment, and the CJS. It made for uncomfortable reading, with racial disparities across the board. Finding that Asian and black households and those in other ethnic groups were more likely to be poor and in persistent poverty. Around one in four children from Asian households are in persistent poverty, one in five children from black households, and one in ten from white households.[7] Disparities were found across the board in Education, Housing, Health, and within the CJS. Mirza was a vocal critic of the report's findings, telling the BBC:

> "Reports like this tend to give an overly negative nature of how ethnic groups are doing in Britain today, and by framing it in terms of racial injustice, it's giving a very misleading picture of why there are disparities, and I think fuelling resentment and grievance, amongst ethnic groups ... to say that this is somehow because of unfair discrimination within the system, or it's because of the colour of their skin, I think it's deeply misleading."[8]

---

4. "Who is Munira Mirza?: Boris Johnson's Controversial Race Inquiry Pick," *THE WEEK*, 16 June 2020.
5. Ibid.
6. Race Disparity Audit, Cabinet Office, October 2017, Summary Findings from the Ethnicity Facts and Figures website (revised March 2018).
7. Race Disparity Audit, Cabinet Office October 2017 (revised March 2018).
8. "What do people think of the Government's race disparity audit?," BBC Daily Politics, 3 October 2017.

Mirza went on to say, "There is discrimination, and there is racism in this country, but I don't think it helps anyone to exaggerate the degree of racism or the degree of discrimination."[9]

As I listened to Mirza, my blood began to boil because although I had to accept that other factors do impact unfair discrimination, I was bemused by her apparent lack of empathy or sufficient understanding of how serious racism can be in impacting people's opportunities. Having experienced racism first-hand and had to deal with the damage it did to my confidence and self-worth, her words were hard for me to stomach. This was only compounded by the fact that someone with such apparently unwavering views on this subject would be heading the Commission on Racial Disparities.

A year later, in 2018, Mirza gave an interview to Francis Foster and Konstantin Kisin on their Channel, Triggernometry on "Multiculturalism, Institutional Racism, White Privilege and Diversity,"[10] in which she stated:

> "There aren't that many ethnic minorities in the arts, academia, or in parts of the media and publishing. But there are longstanding reasons for that. I don't think it's about racism."

In the same interview, she went on to say:

> "We have to get away from the idea that they're not getting in because they're black, and therefore, we have to correct that…and that for far too long, we've racialised these problems."[11]

I cringed as I listened to the confident Mirza talk so openly about a topic with, so far as I could see, no apparent evidence to support these statements. In doing so, I reflected on my attendance at the Young Adult Book Event, where in my quest to break into the fictional young adult publishing world, I sat in on a panel of literary agents who shared their experiences and provided advice on how to prepare a submission to find that all elusive agent. The all-white panel talked about how literary agents need to gel with authors and understand them

---

9. Ibid.
10. "Munira Mirza on Multiculturalism, Institutional Racism, White Privilege and Diversity," Francis Foster and Konstantine Kisin, *Triggernometry*, 9 December 2018.
11. Ibid.

so they can truly invest and promote their work. I looked around the room at the eager budding writers and took on board that I was the only black person there out of a room of over 100 people. As the agents continued to make funny anecdotes about their journey, I felt excluded because none of those agents had knowledge of the lived experience of a black woman. Therefore, what chance did I have of any of them taking a risk on me? A friend at the time told me not to be such a defeatist, but when you are in an environment that is closed off and lacks diversity, it's hard for despondency not to kick in.

I had to do something; I couldn't just stand by and allow Munira Mirza to lead the forthcoming Race and Ethnic Disparities Report without making my point. When it comes to living in Britain, the right to vote makes no distinction between black or white, rich or poor. It provides me with some optimism that no matter how small, I have a stake in what happens in this country. Nothing changes the fact that I have been a part of that democratic process, and when I enter my X in that box, there is a hope that my voice stands for something and that it will be heard. It was at that point I decided I would begin a petition with the website Change.org, which allows people everywhere to start petition campaigns, in which they can mobilise supporters, and work with the decision-makers, as they describe themselves as the "world's platform for change."[12]

My family was cautious, worried that setting out my opinion about Mirza's appointment in writing could place me in hot water with my employers. I told my manager what I intended to do, who was outstanding, stating that as long as I lodged the petition in my capacity as a private citizen, I was permitted to do so. Therefore, on the 17 June 2020, I set up the following:

"Boris Johnson has announced he has appointed his Downing Street aide, Munira Mirza, to lead a commission on racial inequality. The same woman stated it was not racism but 'anti-racist lobby groups' to blame for some of the problems ethnic minorities faced. For hundreds of years, black people's voices have been heard in a whisper, and but for the harrowing 8 minutes and 46 seconds, which ended George Floyd's life, we are now, for the first time, facing a wind of change.

---

12. https://www.change.org/about

Boris Johnson's decision to appoint Mirza is a clear example of how racism devalues the thoughts and feelings of black people; after all the pain, loss, and anger, once again, black people are being sidelined, with decisions being taken out of our hands.

That's why I've started this petition calling for the black community to have a say on who should lead this review and that previous inquiries such as the Scarman Report, the McPherson Report, and the Lammy Report be taken into consideration in its final findings. Racism is a fine-tuned machine made up of many components, and what keeps it functioning with such precision is every individual who stands by and does nothing. If there is to be a review, we MUST have a say in who leads on it.

So, I am asking you to sign and support my petition for the Prime Minister to appoint a lead for this commission with the consultation of the black community because then and only then will we have any faith that it will be conducted fairly and proportionately."

There was a terrifying moment before I pressed "submit" on completion of the process. Despite my fervent belief that it was the right thing to do, I knew that this would place me squarely above the parapet, and I had no idea what that would mean. But I had come too far to stop now, and on returning to work after my break, I had promised myself I would fight for what was right and continue on my journey of self-discovery, so I did it; I submitted the petition.

At first, I shared it with family and friends, who all came back with support and encouragement. Within days, people began to reach out to me on LinkedIn and WhatsApp, saying they had seen my petition and had signed it. Within two days, my petition had reached 1,771 signatures, and people from all over the country signed it. When I realised the interest was growing, I decided to write to my MP, Stella Creasy, asking for her help, and within days her office got back to me, agreeing to help in any way they could.

Within a week of starting the campaign, I had reached over 4,500 signatures. I started weekly blogs to track the campaign's progress and set up a website named citizenscrutiny.org to push the cause. A good friend, a barrister, suggested

I write a letter to the Prime Minister about my concerns. I drafted the following letter on the 23rd of June 2020:

"Prime Minister, you state you want to change, yet you have placed someone at the helm of this commission whose comments make it extremely difficult for the community to accept because any person who does not accept that institutional racism is at the centre of the problem will not be able to report fairly into the issue and will not have the confidence of the public. Therefore, Ms Mirza, the commission, and the Government will be seen as 'biased' due to the various comments referred to above. I discussed my concerns with several peers and found that they were equally concerned over the appointment; with that in mind, I decided to start a petition, but it was more to gather the communities, both whites and blacks, thoughts, and in just five days I have gathered over 5,000 signatures. The message across the board is the same that Ms Mirza's comments on race give them little faith that this commission will be anything but a whitewash due to her predetermined ideals. As a second generation born in a country I love, I want to have faith that things can change, but how can the community believe in effective change if we have no faith in those responsible for leading on it? The unwillingness on the part of Ms Mirza to acknowledge that racism is at the core of the disadvantages we face leaves little hope of our feelings of inequality being met.

Mr Prime Minister, if you genuinely believe that Black Lives Matter, don't just pay lip service to the words; stand behind them. You are in a unique position; you are heading a Government amid this awful pandemic, but you also have within your power the chance to show us that you have faith in the community and its strength of feeling in its opposition to the appointment of Ms Mirza. We ask you, in your own words, to change the narrative and consult with the community to determine how we can bring about a positive change. You and I were born in the same year and month, but our lives could not have been more different. I pray we want the same thing because, Prime Minister, Nothing Changes if Nothing Changes.

Yours sincerely…"

Within a week of sending this letter, I received confirmation from Stella Creasy's office that the letter had been passed to the Prime Minister. But the battle lines had been drawn, and I needed to keep the campaign momentum going. I never received a direct response from Boris Johnson. Still, in July 2020, when signatures had reached 8,790, a press release revealed that the Equality Commission chair would be a former teacher and international education consultant, Tony Sewell, who had previously worked with Boris Johnson in 2013, when he led the then London Mayor's education inquiry into the city's schools, with the Prime Minister stating that Mr Sewell shared his "commitment to maximising opportunity for all."[13]

Sewell has, I should emphasise, an extensive and impressive background within the educational sector, training first to be a teacher at Sussex University and then working for many years in some of London's most challenging schools. He helped transform education in Hackney as part of the team that set up the Learning Trust and the Mossbourne School. This work had national significance, given that it was the flagship of the academy movement. Dr Sewell (now Baron Sewell of Sanderstead CBE) then set up the charity Generating Genius. It has successfully given young people from disadvantaged backgrounds a route to top universities. It was also confirmed that Sewell would be joined by nine others in the group, comprised of representatives from science, education, broadcasting, economics, medicine, policing, and community organizing. They looked at delivering a report on race disparity within the health, education, criminal justice, and employment sectors by the end of 2020, extending to March 2021.

There was no euphoria, no celebrations because because whatever his other and undoubted merits and achievements the selection of Sewell appeared to me and my supporters to rubber-stamp the fact that as well as losing the battle I had also lost the war, believing he sat within the same camp as Mirza. The writing on the wall was when he wrote in *Prospect* magazine in 2010 that "We've given our kids only the discourse of victimhood, and much of the supposed evidence of institutional racism is flimsy."[14]

I felt the rug had been pulled from under me, but I was not about to give up despite what I felt were credible reservations. It was still important to me that I establish what, if any, role Munira Mirza would have within the Race Disparity

---

13. "Charity boss Tony Sewell to head Government race commission," BBC News, 16 July 2020.
14. Sewell, Tony, "Master Class in Victimhood," *Prospect,* 22 September 2010.

Report. Therefore, on the 12 August 2020, I lodged a Freedom of Information request with the Cabinet Office, asking the following: "Has Munira Mirza been appointed to lead the commission? If so, when was this decision made?"

The response I received from the Cabinet Office was that Prime Minister Boris Johnson established the Commission on Race and Ethnic Disparities on the 16 July 2020. The commission was independent and would be chaired by Dr Tony Sewell CBE. It would be made up of ten talented, geographically dispersed, and diverse commissioners.

The sponsoring Minister for this work was Kemi Badenoch, the Exchequer Secretary to the Treasury and Equalities Minister (since 2024 leader of the Tory party in opposition), and they also advised that the commission was independent and supported by the Race Disparity Unit in the Cabinet Office. At the time, it was notable that Munira Mirza was the Director of the No. 10 Policy Unit, responsible for providing policy advice directly to the British Prime Minister. My heart sank. Mirza's powerful influence, aligned with what I'd predicted to be Tony Sewell's approach, left no room in my own mind that she might continue to exert undue influence within the process.

It was a difficult time, and although I felt personally frustrated at Sewell's appointment, I was powerless to do anything about it. But just as I began running out of steam, I got a call that revitalised me. I was contacted by two women called Alicia and Jaden, who had formed an organization called Be That Change (BTC), a local group of men and women based in Waltham Forest, who stood together in fighting against inequality within the borough. They had seen my online campaign and asked if I would meet them.

On a Wednesday evening in late July 2020, I met Alicia and Jaden in a Zoom meeting for the first time. There was an immediate spark between us, as we realised that we were all firm believers in social justice, and wanted to make real change within Waltham Forest. The idea of doing something for my local community was a further step on my important journey and really appealed to me, and although we were all working full-time jobs, we were committed and determined. What was equally important was that it showed me the value of social media in bringing like-minded people together who share a common cause. It also showed the importance of being brave enough to think outside the box. BTC needed someone with legal expertise, and it was wonderful to be a part of something worthwhile.

One of BTC's key objectives was the Windrush Scandal and the ongoing criticism levelled at the Windrush Compensation Scheme (WCS) and the low uptake of the scheme. BTC was also concerned about the lack of trust in the Home Office and low settlement offers being made to victims. Anthony Williams applied for compensation within a week of the scheme opening in April 2019; for the five years in which his life was affected, he was offered approximately £18,000 compensation. In recalling his ordeal, Anthony told journalists: "I gave the youngest part of my life to Queen and country, and I've been treated like a piece of crap by the Government and the Ministry of Defence." Williams was so frightened that immigration enforcement officers would visit him to arrest him and take him to a removal centre that he disconnected the intercom in his flat and never answered the door.[15]

BTC wanted to highlight our concerns and find ways to provide support to residents within Waltham Forest who may have been impacted by the hostile environment and would be eligible for compensation. We knew the starting point had to be with our MP, Iain Duncan Smith, so Alicia set about getting a meeting in place. Her hard work and tenacity paid off, and in September 2020, Alicia, Jaden, and I met with Duncan Smith.

We discussed issues regarding the complex nature of the application forms and addressed the fact that considering the ages of those affected, we would like to establish what support mechanisms are in place for those people within Waltham Forest who may be experiencing difficulties with the completion of these forms and asked if Duncan Smith would contact the council's chief executive and the Home Office to raise these points.

We also placed the option on the table of running a take-up campaign, in which we hoped to involve Waltham Forest Council to try and identify those affected, which we would like to roll out to other boroughs in the future. We requested that Duncan Smith establish from the Home Office if records were kept of residents within Waltham Forest who have been affected and may be eligible for compensation. We were courteous in our manner but robust in our approach to ensure our message got across.

Even though Duncan Smith was polite and personable in his manner, it seemed to me that he had no firm knowledge of the background of the

---

15. Gentlemen, Amelia, "'I feel targeted.' Windrush victim decries compensation delays as racism," *Guardian*, 21 June 2020.

Windrush Scandal, even though his constituency was diverse. But he agreed to raise the issue with the then Home Secretary Priti Patel, and on 8 December 2020 she responded. I am not sure what we expected, but I know what we got: a response consisting of three paragraphs telling us that the way the Home Office collates records makes it impossible to identify residents from individual boroughs. But they are continuing their engagement programme of events reaching out to those who may have been impacted, and they are working with Waltham Forest Council to raise awareness of the Windrush Compensation Scheme. They would be delighted to co-host an engagement event with the council.

On receipt of the letter, BTC set about creating the Windrush Take-Up Campaign; meetings were held to put a strategy in place, working proactively with Waltham Forest Council to access and utilise their communication streams to help BTC's work in exemplifying what living in an anti-racist borough means. I also met with the Windrush officer within Waltham Forest's Citizens' Advice office to see what support we could provide. Flyers were delivered across the borough, and local radio stations also provided support. But no matter how much work we did, the take-up of those coming forward was disappointing, which was quite deflating, but I had always known this would be about trust, and as long as the Home Office held the reins in respect of compensation, people would not feel safe. My work with BTC continued, and despite our disappointment, I would continue to attend meetings, and each of us would ensure regular updates were provided.

It was as if I was on automatic pilot, the day job, chairing the REN, and playing an essential role within BTC, although tiring, was gratifying. Working for Waltham Forest helped strengthen the relationship between BTC and the council when considering how we could all work together to make the borough more equal, including dealing with "hate crime" and education. I was filled with a sense of purpose, which was truly empowering. However, I was unaware that in just a few months, I would be taking a further step into my work with Windrush, which would place me in direct contact with the Windrush victims themselves.

However, throughout my work with BTC and REN, the Race Disparity Report was never far from my mind, and events that followed Tony Sewell's appointment established how well I believe he had been strategically placed in preparing the country for a report that would dilute the devastating effects that racism has had on black people's lives. It also illustrated how far the Government seemed to be prepared to go to push back against the significant impact racism in Britain continues to have.

In October 2020, while evidence was being gathered for the Race Disparity Report, the first debate on Black History Month for five years took place in the Houses of Parliament. In closing the discussion, former Equalities Minister, Kemi Badenoch stood to her feet and told the country that there was a dangerous ideology, one in which black people see "blackness as victimhood and whiteness as oppression."[16]

Victimhood encompasses a belief that a person tends to recognise or consider themselves as a victim of the negative actions of others. And to behave as if this were the case, effectively spending their lives blaming others for their misfortune. In October 2020, Badenoch told *The Spectator*: "The repetition of the victimhood narrative is really poisonous for young people because they hear it and believe it."[17]

In considering what Badenoch had to say, I had to acknowledge the fact that, to her, those of us who speak out against racism that exists within society are effectively poisoning our young people's minds. By highlighting it, we are contributing to these young people's negative perceptions about themselves. I disagree. Young people must know what they need to prepare for their life in our society. I was incensed that she was suggesting that someone like me was using racism as a stick to beat white people with. It was I thought manipulative and cheapened the subject matter's severe nature.

My childhood years were happy, and I could enjoy my life as I played with our white friends. But on the other hand, I was unaware of the "real world" that awaited me. Sometimes, I wished my parents had prepared me and my siblings more because, at least then, we would have been ready for what to expect. The 1960s was a different time and place; maybe my siblings and I were lucky in that we spent our early years on the street as the only black family among orthodox Jews who were never racist to us. Going to school, my class was diverse, with black and white friends. My consciousness of racism was non-existent at that

---

16. Kemi Badenoch, Houses of Parliament Speech, October 2020.
17. "Kemi Badenoch, The problem with critical race theory," The Spectator, Fraser Nelson, 24 October 2020.

time. It is accepted that it may have existed, but I was unaware if it did. Well, at least not until I was old enough to be impacted by it. Were my parents right in concealing it from me?

In his bestselling book, *How To Raise An Anti-Racist*,[18] Professor Ibram X Kendi considered how we talk to our children about racism. This was a question Kendi found himself avoiding as he anticipated the birth of his first child. Like most parents or parents-to-be, he felt the reflex to not talk about racism, which he feared would stain her innocence and steal away her joy. But Kendi argued that it is only by teaching our children about the reality of racism and the myth of race from the earliest age that we can protect them and preserve their innocence and joy.

In December 2020, a further indicator of the possible outcome of the report came in the form of former Minister for Women and Equalities Liz Truss's new approach to tackling inequality, dubbed her "New Fight for Fairness." In this approach, the Government moved away from looking at people with protected characteristics facing inequality, including those from the black community. Therefore, the focus would be related to geographical areas and social backgrounds, effectively sidelining the role racism may play within disparities.

The Conservative's pre-cursor to the release of the Race Disparity Report set in place a Britain in which any reference to racism was seen as victim-led, and that, in line with Truss's Fight For Fairness, planted the seed that those of us who dared to argue about the evils of racism were effectively trying to usurp the rights of a white population. This could not have been further from the truth, but in doing so, everything was in place for the commission to release its findings, which would hit at the heart of the black communities' ancestral pain.

18. Kendi, X Ibram (2022), *How to Raise An AntiRacist*, Vintage.

CHAPTER 16

How I Believe the RDR Diluted the Evils of Slavery, Colourism and Racism

To understand the impact the Race Disparity Report (RDR) had on me, you will need to know more about me and some key events in my life. On 31 March 2021, the report was released in which its chair, Tony Sewell, said:[1]

> "…black people should reconsider the Caribbean experience that speaks to the slave period, that it was not only about profit and suffering, but also about how culturally African people transformed themselves into a re-modelled African Britain."

He also stated: "Some communities were haunted by 'historical racism,' and there was a reluctance to acknowledge that the UK had become open and fairer." Going on to say "Although there is some evidence of bias, often it was a 'perception' that the wider society could not be trusted."[2]

I am haunted when I consider my ancestral past and have nightmares of what would have happened to me if I had been born into slavery. It's even harder when you read the actual experiences of those who lived it, which helped me understand the horrors they faced.

Mary Prince was the first woman to present an anti-slavery petition to Parliament and the first black woman to write and publish an autobiography, *The History of Mary Prince: A West Indian Slave*.[3] The book was a vital part of the anti-slavery campaign. It made people in Britain aware that, although the slave

---

1. Commission on Race and Ethnic Disparities, Report, 31 March 2021.
2. Ibid.
3. Mary Prince (1831), *The History of Mary Prince: A West Indian Slave*, F Westley and A H Davis, University of North Carfolina. Modern edn, *The History of Mary Prince*, Penguin 2000.

trade had been made illegal, the horrors of life on the plantations continued for many people. Mary recalls the harrowing day that she was sold:

> "I was soon surrounded by strange men, who examined and handled me in the same manner that a butcher would a calf or a lamb he was about to purchase. The bidding…gradually rose to 57…The people who stood by said that I had fetched a great sum for so young a slave. I then saw my sisters led forth and sold to different owners. When the sale was over, my mother hugged and kissed us and mourned over us, begging us to keep a good heart. It was a sad parting; one went one way, one another…"[4]

It is unimaginable to begin to grasp how Mary felt as she said goodbye to her mother and siblings. Reading her story reminded me of when I was seven years old. It was Saturday afternoon, and my sister Joyce, who was one year older, was excited because we were going to a concert at a tap-dancing club we belonged to. At first, in the weeks leading up to the event, I looked forward to going, but then, on Saturday, I found out Mum wasn't going with us. I was a mummy's girl; she would take me everywhere, and I loved it. She was an indoor machinist, and I would sit next to her, watching her expertly twist materials into various items of clothing. When I discovered she would not be accompanying us, my heart dropped, but I was too frightened to say anything because the event had been planned for weeks, and everyone was excited.

"What's wrong wid yu? Why yu so quiet," Mum asked in her sweet Jamaican accent as Joyce and I were getting dressed.

"Nothing," I replied, not wanting to say anything about how worried I was that she wouldn't be with us.

When the moment arrived, Joyce and I met the two ladies and other children who had called for us, and Mum stood by the door to wave us off; there was a feeling in the pit of my stomach that I have never forgotten, a fear inside that resulted in a hesitancy to go. But I didn't want to look like a baby in front of the other children, particularly Joyce, who was ecstatic. So, I put one foot in front of the other, and we all started up the road as Mum went back inside and closed the door. Children were all chattering, and Joyce was in the thick of it,

---

4. Ibid.

but the further away we got from our front door, the more uneasy I became. Halfway up the road, I could feel the tears coming. I tried everything to stop them, but with all the will in the world, it was impossible. When the tears did come, it was like a tsunami, I screamed the place down. "I want to go home; I want to go home," I spluttered, and the ladies had no choice but to take me home. When Mum came to the door, I hugged her, closed my eyes, and cried as I squeezed her tightly.

"What is wrong?" Mum asked, concerned. But I was too upset to say anything. She thanked the ladies, took me inside, settled me in the front room, and made me a drink. As soon as I was back in the comfort of my home with Mum, I calmed down and was contented. I didn't care about missing out on the fun my sister and the other children were having; all that mattered was that I was home that Saturday night, safe, with Mum. When Joyce came home, she told me all about what a great time she'd had, which was not surprising because even at the age of eight, my sister was a socialite, whereas I would be happily hidden in my room, reading stories of Milly and Molly Mandy.

At first, I believed Mary's story was similar to any other book I had read, which stirred emotions that left a lasting impression on me. As a teenager, I read the fantastic book, *To Kill a Mockingbird*,[5] a novel by the American author Harper Lee, which dealt with rape and racial inequality, told through the eyes of Scout, a young girl. One of my favourite characters was Atticus Finch, Scout's father, who defended a black man accused of raping a white girl and the dire consequences he and his family faced as a result. But even though it was a book I shall always return to, the feeling was very different from how I felt after reading Mary Prince's story because there was a pain that took hold, which resulted in me reflecting on my own life as a young black girl and then as a black woman. And the reason the feeling was all the more real to me was because I didn't want to feel that way. I tried to brush it off and walk away from it.

Some of us manage to do that, consider the history of slavery as just that, history, and who seem to want to banish it to the back pages of what the RDR referred to as "historical racism."

---

5.   Lee Harper (1960), *To Kill a Mockingbird*, J B Lippincott & Co.

One such person is a lady called Bernadette Raggett, a black woman and adviser of diversity and cultural affairs who received applause from the audience when she told the BBC's Big Question in 2014:

> "…Yes, of course, we know slavery was there, I know bad things happen…you have to move on, we've got to rise above it, and start moving on and think, okay, what are we gonna do in the next hundred and fifty years so that our children can think ah, this happened to my great, great grandfather, but, wow, look what they've done now? We've got to start rising above this and get away from, you owe me this and you owe me that, and going back."[6]

Did Raggett (and some of those who I have mentioned earlier who are of a similar persuasion) have a fair point? Why couldn't I just lay Mary Prince's story in the past and keep it there? When Esther Stanford-Xosei, a representative for the Pan-African Reparations Coalition in Europe, spoke of Intergenerational Transmission of Trauma in the same programme, I was sceptical because I couldn't understand how something that had happened over 150 years before could have an impact on me. But I couldn't ignore how Mary Prince's story made me feel or how it propelled me back to my own childhood experiences. Esther helped me to understand by saying:

> "Slavery and genocide have impacted not only the historical populations that were kidnapped from Africa but also those of us who are the descendants of the enslaved today…Some of the negative legacies that we have internalised of racism, self-hate…prejudice and discrimination, a loathing, in terms of not being proud of who we are…changing our looks to kind of emulate Caucasian beauty ideals, these are some of the real legacies of today in terms of the psychology."[7]

Esther also said "It's a lack of connection; it's a lack of identity, a lack of nationhood, which is what makes us human beings essentially."[8]

---

6. "Should Britain give reparation for Slavery?," BBC, Big Question, April 2014.
7. Ibid.
8. Ibid.

Esther's analysis was distressing for me because, as with the recollections triggered by Mary Prince, her comments took me further down the rabbit hole to a place I wanted to forget. Somewhere that has been rooted not in how white people saw me but in how my fellow black peers saw me and also themselves. Which actually goes back decades and is not just symbolic of how I felt at the time, but how others adorned in a darker skin also felt. Due to the racism of colourism, which stems from slavery, through awful practices created by our black people, which the RDR failed to take into account within its findings.

From 1900 until about 1950, "brown paper bag parties" are said to have taken place in neighbourhoods of major American cities with a high concentration of African Americans. Many churches, fraternities, and nightclubs used the "brown paper bag" principle as a test for entrance. People at these organizations would take a brown paper bag and hold it against a person's skin. If a person was lighter than the bag, he or she was admitted. People with darker skin than a brown paper bag were denied entry. This is still relevant in current-day life, as author Michael Eric Dyson has stated: [9]

"...The brown paper bag criterion survives as a metaphor for how the black elite quite literally establishes caste along colour lines within black life."[10]

Reading about the brown paper bag test put Esther Stanford-Xosei's words into real perspective. The saddest element was that I had to come to terms with the fact that I knew I would not have passed the test, which took me back to myself at thirteen years old.

It was a Friday morning in 1978, a few months before my fourteenth birthday, when the entire year was herded into the large school hall. On arrival, we were surprised to find a group of five teenage black boys dressed in the uniform of a nearby secondary school.

"Come in, girls, sit down quickly," said our head of year, Ms Trent. We did as we were told, but the low whispers around the room clearly indicated our inability to control our excitement. Two boys held guitars, another sat behind a drum kit, holding a drumstick in each hand, while another sat behind a

---

9. Michael Eric Dyson (2007), *Come Hell or High Water: Hurricane Katrina and the Color of Disaster*, New York: Basic Civitas.
10. Ibid.

keyboard, and the tallest of the boys had a microphone commanding centre stage. Ms Trent made her way to the front of the hall.

"Girls, I'd like to introduce you to 'Boys Will Be Boys', an extremely talented group of young people [from a local secondary school] who have been performing for schools across North London. Now, luckily, it's our turn, and I'm sure you are going to make them feel welcome."

My fellow students and I were ecstatic; nothing like this had happened before. I had never seen a live band, and my music experience was limited to watching *Top of the Pops* every Thursday evening on BBC1 and listening to the charts on the radio. It was a real treat to see five boys ready to entertain us. The group started with a one, two, three, and the music began. It was an understatement to say they were brilliant; we were on our feet in no time. Clapping, dancing, and cheering. To us, they were superstars, and it helped that they were all good-looking.

From the moment I walked in, I could not take my eyes off the drummer. He was gorgeous, with a neat puffy afro and a cheeky grin, confidently banging on the drums. It was safe to say I was smitten. I think we were all a little starstruck. When the performance ended, we gave them our seal of approval, cheering and stamping our feet.

We were allowed to stay in the hall and meet the boys when they had finished, but I was too nervous to go over. However, my classmate Sarah confidently made her way over and started chatting to them all. Then I found out that Sarah knew a couple of them, including the drummer. So when we finally filed out to go to lunch, Sarah came over, and she was extremely popular as she was bombarded with hundreds of questions from mesmerised school girls. What are they like? How old are they? Do they have girlfriends? When the furore died, I chose my moment and pulled her aside. I kept my questions very general but must have given more away than intended about the drummer because Sarah suddenly said, "You like Terry; I know you do?"

"No, I don't," I lied. But Sarah was not convinced. She gave me little choice, dragging me along. I was too nervous to go on, so I stopped.

"Come on, man, come on," Sarah pushed, but I couldn't. I was so scared, and besides, Dad had forbidden me from talking to boys, and even though I was at school and knew Dad was nowhere in sight, I couldn't help feeling his eyes on me. Sarah finally relented, agreeing to allow me to wait by the back gates, and she would bring Terry over. That was one of the longest waits of my life, standing there in my school uniform as I prayed that Dad didn't have his watchful eyes over me.

After a few minutes, Sarah returned and called me over to the school gates, where Terry was waiting. My stomach turned inside out as I slowly walked towards him. There he was, this lovely boy dressed in his school uniform, waiting to meet me. But the reaction I got could not have been further away from what I had hoped for. "Oh no, no way, not dat black thing, I couldn't go out with dat!" Terry shouted as he ran back in the direction he had come, with Sarah in pursuit.

It was hard to process what had just happened. I hoped it was a joke, that Terry would come back, laughing and smiling, and be nice. But he didn't, and when Sarah returned, she made an excuse that Terry had to get back to school before quickly making her speedy exit. I felt sick as I walked back through the corridor, and decided to give lunch a miss because, with the way I was feeling, the food would have stuck in my throat. I spent the rest of the day in a daze and prayed for it to end so I could go home. Sitting through French and Geography was torture. My trauma was only made worse because I couldn't tell anyone about it, and for weeks I was terrified that Sarah would reveal what had happened, but no-one in school ever mentioned the humiliating incident. I was glad she had kept my secret.

It would have been easy to think this was just down to Terry not fancying me. After all, I had no experience of boys, and there could have been lots of reasons why he said what he did. I may not have been his type, whether black or white. But I could not get those words out of my mind: "Not dat black thing!" And the more I thought about it, the more I had to accept the awful truth that I was in denial, making excuses for a horrible boy who had hurt me deeply. Had that incident been the only one where the colour of my skin had a significant factor in how people saw me, then maybe, the trauma of that day would have subsided or eased with time.

But to be candidly honest, Terry's words were relatively tame in comparison to what had been levelled at me by other black students, with name calling such as "Trog" and "Ugly black bitch." Names that had become a part of who

I was as a child. Which left me feeling self-loathing. My tormentors took their bullying, based on the colour of my skin, to extremes, creating the name "Munzalezumbe"—a word that they would chant as they followed me to class. Although the word was made up, it made me feel powerless, filled with despair every time I heard it. Munzalezumbe became a label that followed me wherever I went. The most devastating aspect of it all was those words were coming from the black girls who I went to school with, who saw me as ugly and unattractive, and that hurt most of all because they, above all, should know the pain of living in this skin—nothing I say or do can change how that period of my life made me feel. I was in the eye of a storm in which there seemed to be no ending.

But as the decades wore on, and I began to gain more confidence within myself and saw how racism continued to impact black people's lives, I began to understand that it was more about how I saw myself rather than how others saw me. I looked more closely at this stigma attached to those adorned with darker skin. And the deeper I delved into it, the more it became clear that the treatment I received at the hands of my black peers was more about how they saw themselves. Something that had been embedded within them going back hundreds of years was the mythological belief that white and lighter skin was somehow more beautiful and superior.

This myth continues to flourish within modern-day society, with the global skin-lightening products market showing that, in 2017, the global market for these amounted to about 4.8 billion US dollars and is forecast to reach 8.9 billion US dollars by 2027.[11] Figures reveal that 77% of Nigerians use skin-bleaching products, and studies show that the motivation behind it is the desire to appear more important, to look beautiful, and to follow fashion trends.[12]

According to a 2018 nationwide poll on health and lifestyle, 11% of Jamaicans, or roughly 300,000 of the island nation's 2.8 million inhabitants, have used skin-whitening products.[13] Dr Joy DeGruy Leary, elaborated on this point

---

11. Petruzzi, Dominique, "Global skin lightening products market value 2017–2027," *Statista*, 22 February 2024. https://www.statista.com/statistics/863876/global-forecasted-market-value-of-skin-lightening-products/
12. "Skin bleaching in Africa…a public health problem," Analytical Fact Sheet, World Health Organization, African Region, November 2023.
13. "Poisonous beauty: behind the fight to curb skin lightening creams," feature story, Global Environmental Authority, 18 May 2023. https://www.thegef.org/newsroom/feature-stories/poisonous-beauty-behind-fight-curb-skin-lightening-creams

in considering "post traumatic slave disorder" and after conducting six years of research on violence:

> "People can experience trauma indirectly without being involved in the act itself. Chattel slavery was not about a specific event; we are talking about generations of trauma with 'no intervention.' There were no mental health treatments when your child was sold, or you were raped. After slavery ended, did trauma continue, hundreds of years of slavery, no treatment?"

Dr DeGruy Leary says, "African people are extremely resilient; we are profoundly resilient because everything we have done so far is without help." Which has led to what Dr Leary describes as a feeling of "shortened future... self-loathing to hate and despise the reflection in the mirror."[14]

In my late twenties, by then a working woman, I was driving to work; I drove past a school, and there was a black woman holding a little girl's hand. I froze as I recognised her as one of the girls who had bullied me. As I watched her walk through those gates, I wanted to jump out of the car, confront her, and scream at her for all the times she would follow me home from school, taunting me with awful name-calling and relentless attacks on my skin colour. But dealing with colourism as a black woman was two-fold because, on the one hand, you have to face a world in which racism is a part of your life, as you get up in the morning wondering, "Is today going to be a good day" and on the other you cannot ignore the fact that those responsible for causing you so much pain have also shared those experiences. Therefore, I was torn between hating and forgiving because they were dealing with their own demons, but in doing so, they became the very thing they despised.

Mahatma Gandhi said, "The weak can never forgive. Forgiveness is the attribute of the strong." [15] There is truth behind Gandhi's words because it would have been easy to get mad, get even, and expose her for what she was, but what good would that do? It may have provided a short-lived satisfaction within me, but for her daughter seeing her mother confronted in that way, it could have caused irreparable damage. So, I dug deep, looked within myself,

---

14. Dr Joy DeGruy Leary, "Post Traumatic Slave Disorder," Lecture, Terrance Carney. https://www.youtube.com/watch?v=BGjSday7f_8 (accessed 12 January 2022).
15. Ibrahim, Zafar, "Embracing Forgiveness," *Times of India*, 10 September 2020.

and chose to forgive, but although I had forgiven her, I would never forget. As I made my way to work, I thought back to myself as a schoolgirl and how I coped with that time in my life. How did I get through it?

One day was terrible; I was in the changing room after netball practice when they surrounded me and were taunting me, calling me names I don't want to recall; I sat on the bench as the onslaught continued, and, throughout, there was one person who never left my side, my best friend, Janey, a white girl, with striking blond hair and blue eyes. We would stay friends for a long time; I went to her wedding and bumped into her years later in the supermarket when she was with her two daughters. "This was my friend, Pauline," Janey said to her daughters. "We were friends at school." We talked for a while, went our separate ways, and have not seen each other since. I will never forget her, but as children, we find a way to get through; we all do.

At the age of seven-and-a-half years old, famous writer and civil rights activist Maya Angelou became mute; she decided not to speak after suffering the traumatic event of being raped by her stepfather. Maya said:

> "That thing that takes place in the brain of a child, male or female, black or white, when the child encounters catastrophic events, it's so complex and how the child then tries to create some sort of mechanism to cope with that catastrophe."[16]

Maya's coping mechanism was to stop talking following her stepfather being killed after she had revealed what he had done to her. Maya determined that it was "her voice" that had killed him, and had she not told, he would have been alive. She took on all that weight and stopped talking and didn't speak again for five years.

> "I was silent, but I wasn't in silence; all sounds became heightened, I memorised poetry, sonnets of Shakespeare, I fell in love with Shakespeare, Edgar Alan Poe, I memorised whole bits of books…and I loved music and listened to the black American ministers, and because of that intense listening, I believe I have become a good writer."[17]

---

16. Maya Angelou, interview, *Afternoon Plus*, with Mavis Nicholson, Thames TV 1984.
17. Ibid.

Like Maya, I withdrew into myself; I had friends and went to school every day, but I felt lost and ugly. Books such as Jane Austen's *Pride and Prejudice*,[18] which I must have read a dozen times. There was something about Elizabeth Bennett that made her stand out, even at a time when women were no more than just the property of men. Music and films also became my solace.

We had one television set in the house, and on Saturday nights, when everyone was asleep, I would stay up and soak in film after film. My favourites were those showing the harsh realities of working-class life, such as "Saturday Night and Sunday Morning,"[19] depicting a life made up of hard knocks, in which privilege was only available to the chosen few. I loved the fact that despite everything, the main character, played by a young Albert Finney, would ignore the rules, strike out on his own and to hell with the consequences. He took hold of every scrap of life that was available, making no excuses for it. I was also hooked on court dramas, watching programmes such as *Crown Court*, mesmerised by the barristers as they stood to their feet and spoke eloquently and confidently.

I gravitated to characters who were different and would not allow themselves to be constrained by the norms of society. My parents bought me a small transistor radio for my birthday that I would listen to every day, singing along to the Jackson Five, Shalamar, and Donna Summer; I loved Donna Summer, along with one of my all-time favourites, the Beach Boys' "Lady Linda", with its classical slant, along with countless others. We didn't have YouTube or Spotify, so I would make the most of a tune when I heard it on the radio.

Although school could be a terrifying place, there was one topic that I always looked forward to, Drama. Even in primary school, I loved taking part in school plays and would always have a leading role. "Have you ever considered sending your daughter to theatre school?" my primary school teacher, Ms Connerly, asked Mum after one of my many "spectacular" performances. Still, Mum smiled and politely dismissed the idea because, to my parents, drama school was outside their comfort zone, and an acting career was nowhere near to being on their radar. So, I carried my love of acting into secondary school, auditioning for every play, attending after-school rehearsals, and being fitted for costumes. It was wonderful, and the best part was the bullies never joined, so I was safe. I actually became quite a diva, eventually refusing to audition for

---

18. Austen, Jane (1813), *Pride and Prejudice*.
19. "Saturday Night and Sunday Morning" (1960), Director Karel Reisz, screenplay Alan Sillitoe.

principal roles. "Miss, you know I can do this. I've been in every school play. Why are you making me audition all the time?" I asked my Drama teacher, Miss Simpson. When Miss Simpson agreed with me, we shook hands on the matter, and needless to say, for my last year in school, I never had to audition again despite being cast in a principal role, with Mum coming to every performance.

Drama was important because I loved the idea of improvisation, creating your own rules within your characters, and becoming someone else. It was fantastic! On the one hand, I was a confident actress on stage, but as soon as the stage lights dimmed, I was jerked back into the stark reality of being me. I would spend most of my free time hiding in my bedroom, escaping into a world where I could dance, read, and be free. But like Maya, I had no idea that these experiences were shaping me into the person I would eventually become. I loved characters that were different because I knew I was different, and when I found my voice, I took all those thoughts and feelings with me, and the irony is not lost on me that it all started from the cruelty of suffering racism at the hands of my black peers. I suppose that's why the findings of the RDR felt like such a betrayal. I firmly believe that they failed to take account of how destructive racism is and how it creeps into our lives when we least expect it.

My husband, Everton, is a six-foot-two black man who, like me, was born in Britain, first generation to Jamaican parents in the 1960s. A couple of years ago, as a birthday treat, I purchased two tickets to the James Bond Experience, an excellent exhibition featuring memorabilia of Bond films, past and present, near Leicester Square. We took the tube, were both excited to go and were not disappointed; seeing the original cars, scripts, pictures, and clothes was great; needless to say, we took many photos to remember the day. On the way home, we made our way to Leicester Square underground, which was, as expected, very busy on a Saturday evening. Everton had a small rucksack on his back, and I was walking just a little behind him. There was a group of white boys, aged around 18, and as he passed them, one of them said: "There goes another mugger." That comment was met with laughter from his friends.

In overhearing the young man's statement, I had a choice: did I keep quiet or call him out? We'd had a lovely afternoon, and I didn't want to spoil it, but those boys had no right to disrespect my husband or any black man. Besides, I knew Everton well enough to know that he was level-headed and would deal with the situation in a calm and collected way, and as the comment was not directed at me, it was only fitting that I let him know what I had just over-heard. I told him; his face dropped, and I could see he was not amused. He turned and walked towards the group of young men, and asked, "Did one of you say something?"

None of them answered, so he asked again. "I said, did one of you say something?" The collective response was, "No." "I didn't think so," my husband said and took my hand, and we walked away.

The look on those boys' faces, as Everton walked towards them was one of terror, which was totally unjustifiable. He was not threatening them in any way, and calling out their behaviour for a racist comment, which had falsely perceived my husband as a mugger, purely based on the fact that he was a black male. It was crucial to let them know behaviour of that nature will never be tolerated. The failure of the young man who made the statement to own it and the laughter of those with him, making them complicit in that act, showed them up for the cowards they were.

The RDR failed to address the heartbreaking fact that incidents like the one that happened to us that day are a regular occurrence for black men because of dangerous false stereotypical perceptions. My husband regularly relays how he instinctively ensures that when he is walking on the street, in a supermarket, or another public place, he is mindful not to stand too close to a white female because of his height and size, as white women's demeanours change, with them becoming uncomfortable and nervous in his presence.

Across the Atlantic, the American Psychological Association found that peo-ple tend to perceive black men as larger and more threatening than similarly sized white men. John Paul Wilson PhD of Montclair State University and his colleagues conducted a series of experiments involving more than 950 online participants, in which people were shown a series of colour photographs of white and black male faces of individuals who were all equal in height and weight. The participants were then asked to estimate the height, weight, strength, and overall masculinity of the men pictured. Wilson states:

> "We found that these estimates were consistently biased. Participants judged the black men to be larger, stronger, and more muscular than the white men, even though they were actually the same size...Participants also believed that the black men were more capable of causing harm in a

hypothetical altercation and, troublingly, that police would be more justified in using force to subdue them, even if the men were unarmed."[20]

Even black participants displayed this bias, according to Wilson, but while they judged young black men to be more muscular than young white men, they did not judge them to be more harmful or deserving of force. Wilson also stated:

> "We found that men with darker skin and more stereotypically black facial features tended to be most likely to elicit biased size perceptions, even though they were actually no larger than men with lighter skin and less stereotypical facial features … Thus, the size bias doesn't rely on a white versus black group boundary. It also varies within black men according to their facial features."[21]

These were significant factors that the RDR seemed to have overlooked or deliberately omitted, which is concerning because they are relevant to why black men, in particular, can be impacted by this.

In addition, when considering the Race Disparity Commission's comments regarding the slave trade, the United Nations human rights experts in Geneva stated:

> "The Report fails to acknowledge how the legacies of enslavement continue to shape wealth disparities, social stratification and the experiences of people of African descent in Britain."[22]

Kishwer Falkner, the chair of the Equality and Human Rights Commission (EHRC), welcomed the report when it was published, saying it "identifies the varied causes of disparities." However, the EHRC raised fundamental concerns about the approach of the panel appointed by Downing Street as it was conducting its work, stating that the race commission seemed to have been "tasked

---

20. Wilson, John, Paul, Montclair University, Rule, Nicholas O, University of Toronto, Hugenberg, Kurt, Miami University, "Racial Bias in Judgements of Physical Size and Formidability: From Size to Threat," *Journal of Personality and Social Psychology*, published online 13 March 2017.
21. Ibid.
22. United Nations Human Rights, "UN Experts Condemn UK Commission on Race and Ethnic Disparities Report." The experts: Dominique Day (chair), Ahmed Reid, Sabelo Gumedze, Michal Balcerzak, and Ricardo A Sunga III, Working Group of Experts on People of African descent.

with downplaying the role of race-based factors in discrimination which are built into society and instead cherrypicked evidence." Adding, it had tried to "explain away or deny structural racism."[23]

The British Medical Association (BMA) called the RDR a missed opportunity, stating:

> "After due consideration, we firmly refute the overall findings in the Race Report. In particular, they did not find evidence of structural race inequality as a major factor affecting the outcomes and life chances of many of our citizens...they had the opportunity to build on the findings from previous reports and address the underlying causes of racial inequality that led to the Black Lives Matters protests in 2020. Instead, the report's dismissal of evidence of those underlying structural factors may regress rather than progress racial inequality."[24]

I found the language unconscionable because racism runs like an invisible thread throughout society, with no set timeline allowing you to banish it into the past because there are constant reminders telling you it continues to be in the here and now. What was equally concerning regarding the RDR was that the Windrush Scandal was raised just twice in the 258 page report. Mentioning it alongside Grenfell, in its foreword, as an instance "where ethnic minority communities have rightly felt let down." The report goes on to state: "Outcomes such as these do not come about by design and are certainly not deliberately targeted."[25]

The second and only other reference to the scandal comes in the conclusion when it is mentioned in passing as an exceptional example of things going wrong. When I became the chair of the REN, one of the things that stood out most was how staff felt they had been overlooked and undermined. I myself

---

23. Allegretti, Aubrey, "Equality watchdog raised concerns about UK race report, documents show," *Guardian*, 22 April 2021. https://www.theguardian.com/world/2021/apr/22/equality-watchdog-raised-concerns-about-uk-race-report-documents-show (accessed 26 January 2022); https://www.bma.org.uk/media/4276/bma-analysis-of-the-race-report-from-the-commission-on-race-and-ethnic-disparities-june-2021.pdf (accessed 31 March 2021).

24. "A Missed Opportunity," BMA Response to the Race Report, British Medical Association, 15 July 2021.

25. Gentleman, Amelia, "Windrush Campaigners Alarmed by Omissions of No. 10 race report," Guardian, 2 April 2021.

think back to periods within my career where I have been made to feel insignificant and unheard, but it took a long time for me to accept the true fact that I am worth something, I am important, I have a right for my voice to be heard.

As I read the report, turning one page then another, I searched for details of their findings in relation to the Windrush Scandal, but the further into the report I got, the more despondent I became. I finally had to accept that only two references had been made, which skimmed over it. I was so mad. Why is it okay to treat people who have given their best lives to this country with such disdain? To suggest that the Caribbean community was not deliberately targeted when so many of them had been impacted was tragic.

Reading the RDR Final Report only strengthened my belief of how important my voice was and is, not just as Pauline, the lawyer, but as Pauline, the child. To share the story of my encounters with racism, not from a place of victimhood, but from the lived experience of the here and now, which is something sadly missing from the report, that failed to take account of authentic voices of those from the black community living with racism and its impact on our day-to-day lives.

Racism cannot be banished to the history books, and we all must call it out. I was determined to use my voice to show how dangerous diluting the impact of racism can be. It may not be something *I want* to talk about, but it is something *I have* to talk about.

CHAPTER 17

The Windrush Justice Clinic

A mid all the work I was doing inside and outside of my employment, legal heads and voluntary organizations were coming together to provide legal assistance to those in need who had no recourse to financial or legal help. In November 2020, the University of Westminster and London South Bank University brought university law clinics, law centres, community groups, and community members to join forces and launch the Windrush Justice Clinic (WJC). The services provided included advice, assistance, casework, and representation. The clinics provided frontline help. Third-year law students were allowed to work with victims, closely supervised by qualified solicitors, barristers, or accredited caseworkers. Before the clinic's launch, I attended an online meeting where those looking to set up the clinic were present. At the time, I was a mere bystander, interested in the worthwhile work the clinic would be doing. I was in awe of the work of bringing so many professionals together working on a pro-bono basis.

However, early in 2021, I received a call from my former Director of Law, a powerful black woman who I had always looked up to and who has been a light of positivity for me ever since meeting her. Now retired, she contacted me and asked if I would be a supervisor for the WJC. At first, I wasn't sure; it was outside my comfort zone, but she assured me that full training would be given, and my knowledge I had amassed over the last two years of Windrush, and the compensation scheme would stand me in good stead. I agreed, but in doing so, I had to find a way to make it work. Unlike BTC, which had only evening meetings to fit around our day jobs, appointments with victims took place during the day.

I met with the lead lawyer at Westminster Council. Alice was a wonderful woman and was genuinely committed to making the clinic work; she undertook dealing with facilitating and managing the entire thing, which included helping me find my way through Westminster's case management systems, where my appointments and follow-up action would be recorded. Alice also provided excellent training on the key areas and how we would be required to adhere to the supervision of the third year students. Interviews with victims would occur on a rota basis, two to four weekly. As I scrolled through my diary to make room, I could not help thinking back to how history was repeating itself as I recalled my days as a housing benefits officer, persuading my manager at the time to allow me to continue working a 25-hour week, while studying for a full-time law degree. I made it work then and knew I could do the same now.

The Race Equality Network (REN) continued gaining momentum, demanding more time. BTC was also going strong, and following the commissioning of my book *Rice and Peas and Fish and Chips*, due for publication in October 2021, my weekends consisted of edits and re-edits. However, the WJC was essential, and I had to find a way to make it work. Thankfully, my manager was one of the most supportive I have ever had and agreed immediately to me taking the two hours required to attend appointments as long as I could make up my time.

Everything was in place, but the night before my first appointment, I was surprised at how nervous I was. I had been practising law for over 16 years, but up until that point, I had been detached from acting as a legal representative for an individual. Of course, I had championed many causes, but even as a trainee solicitor, I was the administrative legal adviser within the courts. My only contact with the defendant and witnesses was through court service. On qualifying, I became a public sector lawyer; my clients were heads of departments and council officers. When I did deal with defendants, it was mostly through their legal representatives, and in cases where defendants were not legally represented, my engagement with them would be one to two court hearings at most.

I had been shielded from the real world of one-to-one representation of individuals, so I had to prepare myself to face a Windrush victim, where I would advise them. Would I mess it up and crumple at the first hurdle? On the morning of the appointment, I met with the two third-year law students, discussed the case, and advised that I would take the helm. They needed to make detailed notes, as this would determine how we would move forward.

As soon as I began speaking to the individual concerned, I introduced myself and the law students and explained the aim of the appointment.[1] It was as if I were home and had found my calling. This person was not a stranger; we shared a cultural bond, and with that came the empathy required to do the best I could to make sure they received the help they needed. That was not to say that legal representatives who do not share a cultural link with their clients will not do the best they can for them. But for those impacted by the Windrush Scandal, knowing they were speaking to someone who understood their life in Britain helped.

The appointment was intensive, with the victims having to delve into periods of their lives that had been impacted by the unfair treatment they had received. Although I had been qualified for several years, I found that I had to pull on every ounce of my experience to get the person, this individual, to tell their truth. To do that, I had to give them the room to release their pain, which was filled with frustration that had gained momentum over time. Amid the anguish and at the forefront of my mind, I needed to gather as much information as possible because the objective must be to prepare the best case we could to get this person some compensation. The appointment took longer than agreed, but you cannot put a stopwatch on a person's pain. Following the interview, I was sort of shell-shocked because that was my first actual direct experience of seeing, hearing, and advising a victim of the impact the hostile environment policy had in devastating their life. I was conscious that I had read various stories of victims and went into the depths of Anthony Bryan's and Paulette Wilson's cases (*Chapter 11*). Still, although highly distressing, I was removed from any personal involvement, but my first appointment put Anthony and Paulette and everyone like them into real perspective.

The follow-up with the students was telling because when studying law, the only things we think about are lectures, seminars, exams, and more exams. However, being a part of that interview with a Windrush victim gave the students first-hand experience of how significant communication skills and empathy are in law. How it is not just about how good you are on paper and at passing exams.

---

1. An appointment with a Windrush applicant, applying to the compensation scheme, involved the gathering of relevant information to establish if they were entitled to compensation, which would be followed up with further appointments if, based on the information provided, they met the criteria.

The Director of Liberty (the independent justice organization) from 2003–2016, Shami Chakrabarti (now Baroness Chakrabati, CBE, PC) says that of all the rights that exist, the most important is:

> "'The Right to Equal Treatment under the Law.' Lawyers call it non-discrimination translated [into] human empathy. Treating other people as you'd like to be treated yourself. Why is this more important than other rights? Because if we practised empathy, there would be no torture, or slavery or incarceration without charge or trial."[2]

It is accepted that as a lawyer, you must not allow your own emotions to impede you in any way or affect your judgment, but when dealing with a victim who has suffered an injustice that has detrimentally impacted them and their family's lives, it's crucial to build relationships of trust i.e. with individuals, whose core beliefs have been destroyed by a system that has let them down. There was a reluctance to tell their stories because they had been traumatised by their experiences. I came to realise that to truly understand the stark disconnect between the Home Office and the victims of the Windrush (or maybe more appropriately Home Office) Scandal, we had to look at it as a three tier staged process made up of the various components.

First, we have Tier 1, which takes us back to the 1940s to 1960s, when there were jobs for those of the Windrush Generation that were invited here, but even though 87% of men and 95% of women were skilled when they came to Britain, opportunities for the majority were limited to industrial labour, with many working in jobs they were overqualified for. This generation was greeted with a tsunami of inequality in the colour bar, which restricted access to decent housing, employment, and public services. Enoch Powell's "Rivers of Blood" speech in opposition to the Race Relations Bill of 1968, which proposed to make it illegal to refuse housing, employment, or public services to people of colour, has been described as changing the face of politics overnight. Gallop polls at the time showed that 75% of the population was sympathetic to Powell's views. Endemic racism is at the heart of the suffering of the Windrush Generation on the back of this.

---

2. Shami Chakrabarti, Global and Environmental Growth, Human Rights in the 21st Century, TEDx Talks, 2 February 2016.

Then we have Tier 2 because, despite the racism they experienced, the Windrush Generation and their descendants stayed, making Britain their home. But now they have been hit with the additional injustice, stemming from a hostile environment policy, taking the form of the Windrush (Home Office) Scandal. This once again as with the colour bar has denied them access to housing, employment, public services such as healthcare, and the right to British citizenship after spending over 50 years on British shores, despite them having the lawful right to access these services. In many cases this has led to illegal detention and deportation away from their family, life and the only home they have ever known.

Finally, we have Tier 3, which takes us to the Windrush Compensation Scheme (WCS), launched to "right the wrongs" of the devastating effects the Home Office Scandal has had on predominately the Windrush Generation. At the heart of this is the lack of understanding and acknowledgment by those responsible for administering the compensation scheme of the history and pain suffered, which has left victims scared and scarred. This has been compounded by a complicated application process, with the complexity of the form, which in the case of the primary applicant is made up of 44 pages, with accompanying guidance notes of eleven sections. In addition to the forms, a large number of historical documents dating back a number of years are also required, alongside which victims are required to address "Impact to Life." Here they must delve into periods of their lives that had been impacted by the unfair treatment they have received, which is a highly traumatic element of the application process, that on the face of it cannot be justified, once the relevant documentation has been provided in support of the application.

All this baggage is carried into the room on the shoulders of every Windrush victim, but what of those who are not eligible? Not everyone will meet the compensation criteria, but is the pain of mistreatment less traumatic for them? No. But explaining that they do not meet the requirements that will entitle them to financial assistance is never easy, no matter how experienced you are. I was making it work, and with each appointment came a new experience. I had built a good rapport with the students, who were talented, filled with enthusiasm, and excited at being given the opportunity to be involved in the WJC. They also gained invaluable experience in understanding the importance of empathy and doing pro bono work, providing access to justice to those who otherwise would have no legal support.

During this time, I and an excellent barrister also had the idea to hold a seminar entitled "Diversity in Law." For second- and third-year Westminster University law students, focusing on the diverse paths into law, different roles, and specialisms that lawyers and barristers perform, as well as assisting students from diverse backgrounds on the various schemes and initiatives to assist entrants into the profession. The barrister was a white male previously a detective within the police force. He had an excellent eye for detail and was passionate about social justice, we had a great working relationship, and it was wonderful coming together to plan the seminar, which included an essay competition on the law relating to Positive Action, with the winning student gaining one-to-one experience with both myself and the barrister. The feedback was wonderful, with various questions being asked by students throughout. Being able to provide the winning student with the opportunity to attend court and engage with the barrister and myself in respect of the different aspects of our legal profession was truly rewarding.

However, although the WJC and other organizations were doing excellent pro bono work, I couldn't help thinking that despite their worthwhile commitment, we were stagnating. Despite the story breaking, being debated in Parliament, and hitting the headlines once the compensation scheme was set up, people thought "Well that's it. It's sorted," which could not be further from the truth. The Windrush Scandal became the biggest kept secret. Anthony Bryan's story was turned into a one-off BBC film, *Sitting in Limbo*, on 8 June 2020.[3] It was heartbreaking, and many people were in tears. Major channels interviewed Anthony to discuss his experience. But I was surprised and disappointed when the furore began to wane.

I was also conscious that the "Windrush Lessons Learned Review," led by Wendy Williams, had been published just over a year before, on 19 March 2020, in response to the Windrush Scandal. The 30 recommendations made by Williams in identifying the key lessons for the Home Office were all agreed upon by the then Home Secretary, Priti Patel and former Prime Minister Boris Johnson. Following the publication of the report, Williams told Sky News:

---

3.   8 June 2020, BBC, Director, Stella Corradi, Screenplay Stephen S Thompson.

"The Home Office institutionally forgot them [Windrush victims] because of what I have called a culture of ignorance and thoughtlessness as far as the history of the Windrush Generation was concerned."[4] The report also stated that the Home Office had adopted a defensive culture, which made it deaf to those raising genuine concerns.

The review's summary of findings called for tangible evidence that diversity and inclusion were at the department's core, demonstrated by prioritising a meaningful learning development programme. The review also provided that the Windrush Scandal was in part because of the public's and officials' poor understanding of Britain's colonial history of inward and outward migration and the history of black Britons. Williams stated, "Officials must understand the past to inform the present and future of immigration policy."[5]

This element of the report stood out for me because, throughout my legal career, one of the biggest hurdles I faced was the lack of knowledge of my white colleagues of the experiences of living in this skin, which had contributed to making my journey a difficult one. How Home Office officials treated the Windrush Generation emphasised a dangerous ignorance of the contribution this generation and those that had followed had played in re-building Britain following the Second World War. This ignorance led to a continued mistrust of those responsible for implementing the WCS. As I dealt with victims, I could not help drawing parallels between them and my own legal journey. I was reluctant to come forward about my negative experiences because I had no faith that anyone would hear my voice or believe me. I knew that to prove the incidents I faced within the workplace were directly linked to racism would be extremely difficult. Therefore for years, like so many, I suffered in silence, because I felt this was a safer option.

In alignment with this, an inquiry revealed,[6] the low level of applications for the WCS was due to many people struggling with the impossible demands for evidence, poor communication from the Home Office, and a lack of understanding of the issues they faced. For some, the experience of applying for compensation from the Home Office had become a source of further trauma rather than redress, which was all too familiar to a budding lawyer. I

---

4. "Windrush Scandal was 'foreseeable and avoidable,'" Sky News, 19 March 2020.
5. "Windrush Lessons Learned Review," Wendy Williams, 19 March 2020, p. 139.
6. "The Windrush Compensation Scheme," Home Affairs Committee, Fifth Report of Session 2021–22, UK Parliament, 24 November 2021.

remembered my days of struggling to keep my head above water during my training contract before qualifying as a lawyer. I knew that taking on the stress of a legal fight in relation to my treatment would do me more harm than good. I could understand why people were reluctant to enter the lion's den of making compensation applications to those who enforced the immigration laws.

In spite of my misgivings with the process and the Home Office, I knew it was important that everyone entitled to compensation made a claim. I was determined to find a way to encourage and help people to claim. At the time, I had no idea that working for Waltham Forest alongside BTC would give me that opportunity when, in May 2021, I was invited to attend a Windrush Compensation event, hosted by Waltham Forest Council's community engagement co-ordinator, where the Home Office Compensation Task Force would provide a presentation of the compensation scheme.

Importantly, community representatives were also invited to that meeting, and among them was Melinda, the chairperson of the Waltham Forest, Antigua and Barbuda and Domina Twinning Association, who had been granted Home Office funding to launch the Windrush Reach Project (WRP) to raise awareness of the compensation scheme for Waltham Forest residents. The meeting with the task force did not add much to my knowledge, but it enabled me to connect with Melba. Following the meeting and working in conjunction with BTC, I became the sole legal adviser to the WRP. Within weeks of meeting Melba, I was thrown headfirst into drafting letters to MPs such as Stella Creasy and David Lammy about the project in the hope of getting support in spreading the word. As well as drafting the referral form and dealing with queries raised by victims being considered for referral.

Melba and I spoke regularly in preparing the programme for the year ahead, which included six advice and information surgeries, the first three online and the rest face-to-face, three family/intergenerational drop in events. Finally five events with network partners and collaborators, all of which were securely in line with Covid-19 rules. It was a busy time leading up to the official launch scheduled for June 2021. Still, regrettably, the casualty of this decision was my work with the WJC, as it would have been impossible for me to continue.

In June 2021, the year-long WRP was officially launched at the Vestry Museum; it was a wonderful event run by BTC, the Twinning Association, and featured a fantastic exhibition, which through images and regalia, captured

Waltham Forest's Windrush residents who came to the UK from the Caribbean to create new lives from the 1950s to the 1970s. The exhibition curator, Jo Sealy, through 50 contemporary photographic portraits, alongside over 100 personal family pictures, mementos, and oral testimonies, showed how these residents have contributed to the fabric of Waltham Forest in numerous and surprising ways. To launch the event around such a significant exhibition was tremendously moving, and as part of that event I was required to give a presentation on the WRP, key aspects of the WJC, and the role I would play within the former.

It was the beginning of an amazing year. Drafting documents, completing the detailed referral forms, writing articles, and leading presentations at events regarding the WRP was fulfilling. I was doing what I had set out to do, working alongside like-minded people fighting for social justice. However, the ugly face of racism always found a way to rear its ugly head, and this time, it would manifest itself through the world of the not-so-beautiful game.

PART III
USING MY VOICE

CHAPTER 18

Tainting of the England Shirt

On Sunday 12 July 2021, just a few months after the Race Disparity Report was released, I, along with an estimated global audience of 328 million, watched the final of the European Championship between England and Italy from my living room. The entire country took pride in the fact that the England team, managed by Gareth Southgate, was the most successful in over 50 years. The final took place in Wembley Stadium before a crowd of 67,163 people.

I remember almost losing my voice as my husband, his best friend, and I jumped and screamed in a state of pure euphoria when England's Luke Shaw opened the scoring in the second minute of the match. The fastest goal ever scored in a European Championship final. The entire country went crazy; it was a wonderful feeling. However, our excitement turned to dismay when Leonardo Bonucci equalised midway through the second half. The final score after extra time was England 1, Italy 1, and the only way left was a penalty shoot-out. My stomach turned inside out as I watched each player take the spot kick. If it was torture for me, I cannot imagine what it must have been like for them. As the England players planted their ball on the spot, I whispered, "Please don't miss, please don't miss."

The shoot-out occurred at the goal behind which many England fans were situated. Both sides' first penalties (from Berardi and Kane) were successful. England goalkeeper Pickford then saved from Belotti before Maguire converted his kick to give England a 2–1 advantage. Bonucci scored to level the shoot-out at 2–2 before late substitute black player Marcus Rashford hit the left-hand post with England's third penalty. Bernardeschi gave Italy the lead again with a low shot down the middle before England's other late substitute, black player Jadon Sancho, had his shot to the right saved by Donnarumma. Jorginho stepped up to take the possible match-winning penalty for Italy. But his shot was saved by

Pickford. With the score 3–2 to Italy, black England player Bukayo Saka took England's fifth penalty, looking to equalise and send the shoot-out to sudden death. Still, Donnarumma dived to his left and saved it to secure Italy's second European Championship. The final score in the shoot-out: Italy 3, England 2. It was devastating to see the distraught looks on the three black players' faces as they cried in their teammates' arms.

But along with the awful disappointment, there was a look of fear in our eyes as we stared at each other in that room because we instinctively knew what was going to happen. We were only too aware that those black players and the black community as a whole would have to face the wrath of the racists. When the final score was announced, black people nationwide were on high alert. One of my black colleagues at work made sure their teenage child was accompanied to school the following day, and these types of behaviours happened throughout the black community.

The racists did not disappoint. After the game, England players Saka, Sancho, and Rashford were subjected to racist abuse online after missing penalties in the shoot-out. The three were immediately targeted with racist language and emojis on their social media accounts.

In a statement, the Football Association said:

"We could not be clearer that anyone behind such disgusting behaviour is not welcome in following the team. We will do all we can to support the affected players while urging the toughest punishments for anyone responsible. We will continue to do everything we can to stamp discrimination out of the game. Still, we implore the Government to enact appropriate legislation quickly so this abuse has real-life consequences. Social media companies need to step up and take accountability and action to ban abusers from their platforms, gather evidence that can lead to prosecution, and support making their platforms free from this type of abhorrent abuse."[1]

During the three days after the game, Saka, Sancho, and Rashford expressed their gratitude for the support they received on their social media accounts.[2]

---

1. "FA condemns racist abuse of players following England's Final loss," Reuters, 12 July 2021 (archived from original on 12 July 2021; retrieved 12 July 2021).
2. https://scroll.in/field/1000324/full-text-love-always-wins-saka-joins-sancho-rashford-in-issuing-statement-against-racial-abuse (accessed 27 January 2022).

Rashford apologised for his penalty miss but said he wouldn't apologise for who he was and where he came from.[3] Sancho said: "Hate will never win" and "As a society, we need to do better and hold these people accountable."[4] And that he "knew instantly the kind of hate" he would receive.[5]

I contemplated where I and the black community could go from here. It seemed that British society took two steps forward, but the racists were determined to push us four steps back. White colleagues at work were supportive and ridiculed the behaviour of what they described as a few small-minded racist individuals. But I didn't see it that way because one racist was one too many for me, and their evil actions only emphasised how dangerous the Race Disparity Report was in dumbing down racism within the UK. What was equally concerning was many of these people were concealed behind social platforms, so as a black person I had no idea who they were. It was likely that many of them worked with black people, smiling and laughing with black colleagues while at the same time holding racialised ideals.

I would never cast aspersions on any of my colleagues in Waltham Forest, who have never been racist to me in any way. Still, we needed to ensure when it comes to the fight against racism, we take appropriate action, to ensure our voice is heard. Therefore, during that week, I put pen to paper and drafted the following statement on behalf of the REN:

"STATEMENT FROM RACE EQUALITY NETWORK: THE TAINTING OF A PRIDE IN WEARING AN ENGLAND SHIRT

In January 2020, Laurence Fox was applauded by an audience on Question Time as he told Britain, 'We are the most tolerant lovely country in Europe.'

In December 2020, the Minister for Women and Equalities Liz Truss in her Fight for Fairness speech stated, 'Too often the Equality debate has been dominated by a small number of unrepresented voices, and by those

---

3. "Marcus Rashford: England striker 'wont apologise' for who he is after receiving racist abuse," 13 July 2021, BBC Sport. https://www.bbc.co.uk/sport/football/57814154 (accessed 27 January 2022).
4. "Jadon Sancho: England forward says 'hate will never win' in response to racist abuse," 14 July 2021, BBC Sport. https://www.bbc.co.uk/sport/football/57840951 (accessed 27 January 2022).
5. Ibid.

who believe people are defined by their protected characteristics and not by their individual character.'

In February 2021, Priti Patel told LBC, she did not agree with people taking the knee in support of Black Lives Matter, stating 'There are other ways in which people can express their opinions.'

In March 2021, the Report on Race Disparity, commissioned in the wake of the Black Lives Matter and the protests that erupted following the tragic death of George Floyd, concluded that the UK has become a 'more open society.' The Commission's Chair, Tony Sewell, told Britain, 'Some communities were haunted by "historical racism, and there was a reluctance to acknowledge that the UK had become open and fairer,"' going on to state that 'although there is some evidence of bias, often it was a 'perception' that the wider society could not be trusted.'

This week, we watched as those perceptions manifested themselves into racist abuse via social media, directed at three black England players, Marcus Rashford, Jadon Sancho and Bukayo Saka.

Priti Patel stated she was 'disgusted' despite refusing to criticise fans who booed the England team for taking the knee in protest against racial injustice.

This week a petition created by football fans Shaista Aziz, Amna Abdullatif and Huda Jawad has reached almost one million signatures. The petition calls for the Football Association (FA) and the Government to work together to ban 'all those who have carried out racist abuse, online or offline, from all football matches in England for life.'

REN members support this petition in the stand against racism and urge the Waltham Forest Chief Executive to continue to work with us in fighting the evils of racism, which is not limited to the football pitch but is manifested within an inequitable society, where life choices and opportunities are limited.

The race disparity report states that life becomes harder if people from ethnic minority backgrounds absorb a fatalistic narrative that says the deck is permanently stacked against them.

In October 2020, Marcus Rashford stated he was 'honoured and humbled' after being awarded the MBE at the age of just 22 in recognition of his services to vulnerable children in the United Kingdom during the Covid-19 pandemic. And this year he stood alongside his fellow black players Jadon Sancho and Bukayo Saka, who showed no hint of a fatalistic narrative, in being part of the most successful England Team in over 50 years.

Tony Sewell stated that for some groups, historical experience of racism still haunts the present; that's because it is and continues TO BE PRESENT. The question is how can we forget the past where the pride of black players wearing an England shirt is tainted by the 'N' word, and statements referring to Bukayo Sako as a runaway slave being captured by his master continually force us to remember.

Pauline Campbell
Co-chair of the Race Equality Network
London Borough Waltham Forest."

REN's statement was placed on Your News, a Waltham Forest update sent to every employee within the council. Following its publication, a number of staff approached me to rubber stamp its content. A few weeks later, I was shopping, and a black woman approached me. "I am really sorry to bother you, but we have never met. I just wanted to tell you I have been following you on LinkedIn and love everything you are doing, and I loved your statement about football." A conversation struck up between us, which lasted for so long my husband, who was waiting in the car, came in to find out what had happened. When we parted, we hugged, and the woman went on her way. The conversation stayed with me for the rest of the day as I began to see my voice's impact.

I remember the look on the woman's face when she approached me; she was nervous, which was probably due to her not knowing how I would have responded. I had no idea where she worked or her background, but what stood out was she was an ordinary person, just like you or I, who felt empowered enough to share her thoughts with me on the work I was doing. This not only reinforced my resolve it also strengthened it, which illustrated how powerful our voices can be. I was "fulfilling the highest, truest expression of myself."[6] When the project ended in April 2022, Melba and I continued to help people who approached us because although funding had dried up, the problem did not simply disappear; people still needed help.

As a member of the WJC, BTC, and now the Windrush Reach Project, I looked at what the Government was doing to ensure the legacy of the Windrush Generation was being recognised in accordance with Wendy Williams' "Lessons Learned Review." What could they do to dispel my anger and despondency?

---

6. Oprah Winfrey, Commencement Address to Class of 2012, Spelman College, Mississippi, 20 May 2012 (accessed 2 January 2024).

CHAPTER 19

The Olive Branch

In June 2018, Theresa May, former Prime Minister, invited men and women from the Windrush Generation to No. 10 Downing Street to celebrate the 70th anniversary of Windrush. I watched as black people walked through the doors of No. 10, dressed to impress, following May's announcement of an official annual Windrush Day, which would take place on June 22, along with the establishment of a Windrush Commemoration Committee to consider how best to create a permanent, fitting tribute to the Windrush Generation and their descendants. Baroness Floella Benjamin, selected as chair of the committee, who attended the event, said her heart was leaping for joy.

Others were more sceptical, with Professor Kehinde Andrews stating:

> "As Home Secretary, she pursued the hostile environment policy, replete with 'go-home-vans,' deportations and the very immigration checks from the private sector that blew up into the Windrush Scandal."[1]

Gus John, an academic and equality and human rights campaigner, refused his invitation along with other invitees, stating,

> "I do not believe that the Prime Minister is entitled to the magnanimity of those misguided folk who might well be happy to attend her Windrush anniversary celebration. I stand with those who suffered detention, deportation, and mental ill-health, some of whom even now face an earlier death as a result of being denied access to health services on account of the hostile

---

1. Andrews, Kehinde, "A national Windrush Day? Theresa May has some nerve," *Guardian*, 18 June 2018.

environment policy. It would be a shameful betrayal to them all to accept the invitation to Downing Street."[2]

In June 2022, Basil Watson's sculpture, the national Windrush Monument, was unveiled at Waterloo Railway Station. The statute backed by £1m of Government funding, portrays three figures, a man, woman, and child dressed in their Sunday best. Climbing a mountain of suitcases hand-in-hand. Members of the Windrush Generation and the Duke and Duchess of Cambridge gathered at Waterloo for the unveiling. Queen Elizabeth II also sent a message to mark the occasion: "It is my hope that the memorial will serve to inspire present and future generations."[3] Floella Benjamin stood on a podium and announced: "It will act as a symbolic link to our past and a permanent reminder of our shared history and heritage for generations to come."[4]

But as the publicity photos were being taken, with school children standing alongside the royal family, I reflected on a past in which I was described as a wide grinning picaninny by Enoch Powell, how as a teenager I watched the streets of Brixton light up against social injustice, how at 21, I found police on every street corner following the riots in Tottenham that ended the life of PC Keith Blakelock. I considered how I wept at the racist murder of Stephen Lawrence, and later in my life, along with the rest of the black community, was fearful for the safety of three outstanding young black England footballers, racially abused for missing penalties in a European Cup Final. The final blow was that I was only too aware that justice still eluded so many Windrush victims.

The Windrush Monument was supposed to provide the Windrush Generation, of which I was a part, with a sense of recognition for the important role my parents and those like them played in rebuilding Britain following the Second World War. But I could not help thinking that, as with the tragic murder of George Floyd, which lit a beacon across the world in the fight against racism, would the monument have even been considered if the Windrush Scandal had never happened? Why did it take the devastation of so many people's lives for the black Caribbeans' contribution to Britain to be acknowledged? This

---

2. "Why I'm turning down Theresa May's invitation to celebrate Windrush," Gus John, *Guardian*, 21 June 2018.
3. Khomami, Nadia, "Windrush Generation 'Moved to Tears' as Monument Unveiled in London," *Guardian*, 22 June 2022.
4. Ibid.

led me to a point where I questioned the very heart of my Britishness, and I am not alone.

The Black British Voices (BBV) survey revealed in October 2023 that only 12% of black people were definitely proud to be British, and less than half (49%) felt British at all.[5] The survey showed the impact that lived experiences of racism have on identity and belonging. Finding that claiming British identity has been a complicated and multifaceted experience. One BBV participant aptly described choosing to call themselves black British as "a journey, it's not a destination."[6]

The participants' descriptions were correct when applied to my own experiences. My education, working life, studying law, training, qualifying, and now being part of the legal profession was literally a journey filled with a number of twists and turns, in which being black played a significant role in how I have been perceived and treated. I accept that within the world of law, being a woman from a State school would overlap with some of the inequalities I was presented with. But by far, my colour has been and continues to be the dominating feature in the negative experiences I have had.

Renowned black writer and poet Benjamin Zephaniah, who sadly passed away in 2023, told BBV that his affinity to British identity was more appreciation than pride, saying:

> "We have to understand what a privilege it is to have a passport to a country. I know people with no passport, no country, and nowhere to return to…When all goes wrong, we can come to Britain. There is something about when I'm away and especially if I'm getting on a British plane, when I'm coming back, I think this is home. I've had the opportunity to leave here [Britain] and I haven't left here."[7]

Like Zephaniah, I have travelled abroad with my British passport and have never questioned that Britain is my home on my return. But despite that, I would never feel comfortable waiving the Union Jack or the St George's flag. This isn't because I don't appreciate the significance of what they represent to

---

5. Black British Voices: i-Cubed, *The Voice*, University of Cambridge, October 2023.
6. Ibid.
7. Ibid.

British people, they have been described as "unifying objects to bring its people together. A symbol holding the incredible power to unify, whether that's a competitive nudge in a sports game, a nation celebrating its history, rulers, and freedoms together, or a sign of solidarity for a nation in times of violence."[8]

In 2018, Dr Kehinde Andrews, a Professor of Black Studies at Birmingham University, told *Good Morning Britain* that the "English flag (St George's flag) isn't just a symbol of racism, it may be the primary symbol of racism in this country because of how it's been adopted and co-opted by [the] far right, and my mum's generation it was Keep Britain White…in my generation, it was a National Front telling me to go home, and now you've got the English Defence League, the British National Party, and all these other groups."[9]

Although I agree with Kehinde in relation to how extreme far-right groups have misappropriated British flags, I cannot forget how, throughout my life, the Union Jack, in particular, has held a different meaning. I remember watching Daley Thompson, one of the greatest decathlete British black athletes the world has ever seen, with four world records, two Olympic gold medals, three Commonwealth titles, and wins in the World and European Championships. I and millions watched as Daley, proudly wrapped the Union Jack around his shoulders. In 2000, I also watched as British black athlete Denise Lewis became the only woman to win a medal from athletics, walking away with a gold medal in the heptathlon at the Olympic Games in Atlanta. She was twice Commonwealth Games champion, and European Champion in 1998, and won World Championships silver medals in 1997 and 1999. Denise stood with pride after her phenomenal wins, holding the Union Jack and the St George's flag, celebrating her victories. Like myself, Denise was born in Britain to Jamaican parents, who had made a life for themselves on British shores.

In commemoration of 2023 UK Black History Month's theme was "Celebrating Our Sisters." Denise said when speaking of her achievements:

> "I think representing Team England is such a big deal,…there's a sense of unity that's really powerful, and it gives you a lot of confidence. I could never have imagined what it would be like fast forwarding to 20 years from competing in 1998 to standing as President at the Gold Coast for Team

8. Why are flags important? Ship's Log, Shipwreck Treasure Museum, 14 June 2022.
9. "Is the English Flag Racist?," *Good Morning Britain*, 23 April 2018.

England; it was just remarkable; it was one of the proudest experiences I could ever have imagined."[10]

Denise went on to say:

"The murder of George Floyd and the ramifications of that has forced everyone to really look at themselves, not only our white counterparts but us as black people. I don't think we've been comfortable enough sharing some of those stories and putting them in the public domain. I do think it's really powerful now that we can each hear how we have been affected, or what has shaped us, or how we've had to dig deep to rise above some of the racism."[11]

I like Denise Lewis and countless other British black people, am a product of British society and all it encompasses, part of which are those who wish to exclude me from the right to be recognised as British. This by hijacking the true meaning of flags that should bring people together, rather than tear them apart, which provides a painful reality to the good, bad and the ugly aspects of what it means to be black and British.

But something was profoundly clear in how I viewed my bittersweet life as a black British woman, and that was I wanted to be a part of change; standing still was not an option for me, becoming a lawyer, writing my books, the various roles held in respect of Windrush was a testament to that. However, in late 2022, I would embark on a journey with a nemesis that, although I would never meet, would not only cause waves within the Windrush Compensation Scheme but strike at the heart of key recommendations of Wendy Williams' "Lessons Learned Review."

---

10. Dame Denise Lewis, "Why Black History Month Matters," 26 October 2023. https://teamengland.org/news/dame-denise-lewis-why-black-history-month-matters
11. Ibid.

CHAPTER 20

The Cat and the Canary?

In December 2022, I was building a decent following on LinkedIn, the world's largest professional network on the internet. I met several people and made some great contacts within the platform. Some of which included recruitment agents. However, even though I was not looking to leave Waltham Forest, I had an ear to the ground for opportunities. In December, I found what seemed to be the perfect job. The Home Office advertised for a lead part-time non-executive director to work on the Wendy Williams' "Lesson Learned Review's" recommendations, stating: "We are working hard to support those affected by the Windrush Scandal and transform the culture within the department. Our work and our relationships are underpinned by our values: being respectful, compassionate, courageous, and collaborative."

I was highly interested in this role, not just because it was possible to do this alongside my work as a senior lawyer, but as a descendant of the Windrush Generation and a pro-bono lawyer for Windrush victims, I felt in a role such as this I could make a real difference. I could add my voice from the inside. However, I knew I would have to proceed with caution, particularly bearing in mind that just two years before, the most senior black Home Office employee in the team responsible for the Windrush Compensation Scheme had resigned. They had described the scheme as systemically racist and unfit for purpose. It was also revealed that a separate set of complaints about discrimination within a different Home Office team researching the causes of the Windrush Scandal led to an earlier internal investigation. About 20 members of staff working on the independent Windrush "Lessons Learned Review" by Wendy Williams were interviewed by a Civil Service equality, diversity and inclusion officer after allegations of racially discriminatory treatment were made by minority ethnic staff members.

Alexandra Ankrah, a former barrister who worked as head of policy in the Windrush Compensation Scheme, said she resigned because she lost confidence in a programme that she alleged was "not supportive of people who have been victims" and which "doesn't acknowledge their trauma."[1]

Several proposals she made to improve the scheme were rejected, she said: "The results speak for themselves: the sluggishness of getting money to people, the unwillingness to provide information and guidance that ordinary people can understand."[2] Ankrah was troubled by the fact that several Home Office staff responsible for the compensation scheme had previously helped implement the hostile environment policies that had caused claimants so many problems.

Despite my reservations, I decided that we were now two years on, and I owed it to myself not to back away from a challenge that my exploits over the past few years had instilled in me. So, I downloaded the job pack, which I read with interest. However, I stopped dead in my tracks when it became apparent that my direct line manager would be Suella Braverman. I cannot understand why it would not have occurred to me then that she would be my line manager as the former Home Secretary.

I was faced with a difficult decision; on the one hand, I knew that the only way to impact change is to be at the table at which decisions are being made. But on the other, I also had to consider that at the helm of that table would be a woman who when holding the role of Attorney General stated:

> "Diversity zealots have created a dangerous new religion—we must be serious about taking them on…It is all too easy to view the past through the prism of the present and then use the new orthodoxy to settle old scores. Today that orthodoxy is called Diversity, Equality and Inclusion."[3]

The deadline for the application was 3 January 2023, and I must have read it 100 times, but each time I went to complete it, my hands froze because it seemed difficult to understand how the views of Braverman could ever be aligned with that of the "Lessons Learned Review," which determined that

---

1. Gentleman, Amelia, "Black official quit 'racist' Windrush compensation scheme," *Guardian*, 18 November 2020.
2. Ibid.
3. Braverman, Suella, "Diversity Zealots Have Created a Dangerous New Religion—We Must Get Serious About Taking Them On," *Daily Mail*, 3 August 2022.

diversity and inclusivity was an essential part in changing the defensive culture within the Home Office. The closing date was fast approaching, and I knew that there was no time to procrastinate, but integrity and values were important to me, therefore before completing the application, on 16 December 2022, I made a Freedom of Information request to the Home Office, in which I asked the following:

"I am writing this in response to the role advertised for the Home Office Lead Non-Executive Director to work on the Windrush Lessons Learned Review. The job pack states:

The Review's summary of findings called for tangible evidence that diversity and inclusion were at the department's core, demonstrated by prioritising a meaningful learning development programme. Page 139 of the Review provides that the Windrush Scandal was in part because of the public's and officials' poor understanding of Britain's colonial history of inward and outward migration and the history of black Britons. Going on to state, 'Officials must understand the past to inform the present and the future of immigration policy.'

During her role as Attorney General, Suella Braverman made the following statement for the *Daily Mail*:

'Diversity zealots have created a dangerous new religion—we must get serious about taking them on' and went on to state: 'It is all too easy to view the past through the prism of the present and then use the new orthodoxy to settle old scores. Today that orthodoxy is called 'Diversity, Equality, and Inclusion.' I also note that while holding the role of Attorney General, Braverman scrapped diversity training within her department.

This statement is extremely worrying because the Windrush generation and their descendants have been impacted by racism since arriving in Britain in the 1940s through organizations such as the White Defence League, decades of racist rhetoric from Enoch Powell beginning with his Rivers of Blood Speech, as well as Powell becoming the go-to person on race during this period, the National Front, discriminatory employment practices. Even within the Home Office and the Civil Service itself, there is a proven lack of representation of black staff at senior levels. Having worked with several Windrush Victims, as well as conducting seminars and workshops on the historical importance of Windrush and the World of Politics, I find it hard to fathom how we can have any confidence in this Non-Executive role with Suella Braverman at the helm because the incorporation of these recommendations requires 'mutual trust and respect' on the part of all parties. As part of the recruitment process, due diligence, including social media checks, will be undertaken on the appointable candidate. The problem I am faced with is, bearing Suella Braverman's comments in mind, what due diligence has been conducted regarding her suitability to oversee this role."

Bearing my request in mind, I asked if the Home Office would consider extending the closing date to allow time for their response.

In December 2022, I wrote to the *Law Society Gazette's* commentary and opinions page, and on 21 December 2022, my commentary "Windrush 'Lesson Learned' Review Appears Doomed to Fail,[4] with Suella Braverman at the Helm" appeared. In writing the commentary, I was pre-empting the inevitable from the Home office, which, on the 19 January 2023, after the closing date had passed, provided the following response to my Freedom of Information Request: "The Home Office is unable to comment on the statements and actions of the Home Secretary."

Less than a week later, while still licking my wounds at being disregarded, the Home office published an update on the "Lessons Learned" recommendations in which Braverman had made a decision not to proceed with Recommendations 3 (Run Reconciliation Events); Recommendation 9 (Introduce Migrants' Commissioner); Recommendation 10 (Review the Remit and Role of the Independent Chief Inspector of Borders and Immigration (ICIBI)) in their original format.

The frustration was immeasurable. It seemed no matter how hard I had tried, those who held power were determined to close their minds to real change. The most tortuous aspect was seeing Suella Braverman placed at the forefront of

---

4. Campbell, Pauline, "Windrush 'Lesson Learned' Review Appears Doomed to Fail," *Law Society Gazette*, 21 December 2022.

Wendy Williams' "Lessons Learned Review". This was tantamount to putting a canary in the care of a cat. I could do nothing to stop it. I was also curious about the non-executive director role, which seemed to have dropped under the radar, with no announcement of whether anyone had secured the position. I gave serious thought to drafting another Freedom of Information request to find out. Common sense helped me to see that I had much better things to do than expend precious time and energy on a job that could only be described as a poisoned chalice, which came from the starting point of three of the key recommendations that I would have been required to work towards implementing being scrapped at the first hurdle. So, I did the sensible thing: I let it go. I learned throughout my journey that time is precious, and you need to invest in how you utilise it carefully. Of course, the Home Office failed to respond appropriately in my view, but that said more about them than it did about me.

However, in June 2024, the High Court found that Braverman's decision to scrap Recommendations 9 and 10 was unlawful because it breached the public sector equality duty. However, it was disappointing that the High Court stated Braverman had not acted unlawfully regarding Recommendation 3, which required running reconciliation events. In which victims could speak freely to senior Home Office officials about how the Windrush Scandal detrimentally impacted a victim's life and feel they have been listened to.

Finally, and ironically, following the publication of my book *Rice and Peas and Fish and Chips*, I was invited to attend as a guest author with the Civil Service to talk about my experiences. But just a few weeks before I was due to appear, I was contacted by a civil servant and politely informed that my invitation had been withdrawn because I had failed the Civil Service's due diligence test. I was simply disinvited, and no explanation was ever provided. This leaves me wondering why to this day.

CHAPTER 21

My "Badge of Honour"

I was nervous at being given the old "heave ho" by someone from the all-powerful Civil Service. I wondered what checks had been conducted for them to make their determination and what other scrutiny was being undertaken concerning me. It was an unsettling feeling because it wasn't what they did say. It was what they didn't say that gave me reason for concern, as it made no sense that they would make such a decision and fail to provide me with any explanation. It was impossible not to make comparisons between their treatment of me and the Windrush victims, who were condemned, and treated as illegal residents, through no fault of their own. Of course, there was no suggestion that I would have been carted off in the middle of the night and held in detention. Still, I thought back to the Windrush victim, Anthony Williams (*Chapter 15*), who was so frightened that immigration enforcement officers would visit him to arrest him and take him to a removal centre that he disconnected the intercom in his flat and never answered the door.

Even though this did not happen to Anthony, the threat was natural to him because the track record of the Home Office showed it could have happened at any time. Therefore, I felt justified in my uneasiness, which could only be described as driving past a speed camera and suddenly seeing a flash, resulting in you checking your speed. When you then realise you are just a little over, worrying for weeks waiting for the dreaded ticket to arrive, or worse, points to be added. I never received a ticket or points, but I would be on tenterhooks for those few weeks, hoping for the best but waiting for the worst. There were also concerns about how this may have affected my legal career, how lawyers face stringent scrutiny, and how the Civil Service's decision would impact my reputation as a lawyer. Did their checks include investigations into my professional life, employers, and so forth?

But even though I was apprehensive during the weeks following their decision, my mindset had not changed. I continued to work proactively as chair for the Race Equality Network and issue posts on my LinkedIn regarding issues that gave me reason for concern. Only then did I truly understand my commitment to equality and the fight for all voices to be heard. I had been frightened to use my voice for so many years that I was determined never to allow anyone to stop me from using it again.

In withdrawing their offer, the Civil Service had done me a favour because they made me take a long hard look at what I stood for. When faced with the prospect of being under their spotlight, it would have been understandable for me to conclude that enough is enough; I have done my bit; I can now step back and get on with the rest of my life under the radar, where it's safe. But what kind of a lawyer and, more importantly, person would I become in making that decision?

Black Human Rights lawyer and activist Kimberley Motley travelled to Afghanistan to train Afghan lawyers for nine months and talked to hundreds of people who were locked up. During her talks with businesses and the people, Kimberley saw how laws meant to protect them were being underused. At the same time, gross and punitive measures were being overused. These put her on a quest for justness, which she defines as using laws for their intended purpose, which is to protect. Kimberley became the first foreigner to litigate in Afghan courts, who realised the lack of justness was not just a problem in Afghanistan, it was a global problem. But in doing so, Kimberley said,

> "And while I originally shied away from representing human rights cases because I was concerned about how it would affect me both professionally and personally, I decided that the need for justness was so great that I couldn't ignore it."[1]

So, she started her pro-bono work in Afghanistan.

Reading about the fantastic work of Kimberley Motley helped to put things into perspective, with her apt description of justness and why, despite reservations on her part, it was impossible to ignore the injustices being faced by the

---

1. Kimberley Motley, "How I defend the rule of law," TED, 27 October 2014. https://www. youtube.com/watch?v=Td2hfdXQ5x8

Afghan people. She was right in her classification of justness that the role of laws is to protect, and it hit home how, in Britain, when applied to those affected by the Windrush Scandal, those laws had the opposite effect. With that in mind, I allayed my fears of "Big Brother watching me". I saw it as a positive because it meant that I must be doing something right, and rather than it be damaging to me I saw their rejection as a badge of honour. One that placed me squarely in on the peg of a lefty lawyer and all that it entailed.

I picked up the gauntlet in the fight against inequality, raising awareness of the social injustice suffered by Windrush victims and tackling the importance of Equality, Diversity and Inclusion within and outside the workplace. My work with the REN, BTC, the WJC, and the WRP, in conjunction with the publication of *Rice and Peas and Fish and Chips*, was like a melting pot that invigorated me, giving me a real purpose, culminating in my social justice work becoming a prominent aspect of my life.

It seemed there were not enough hours in the day, as I worked around the clock to ensure legal deadlines were met within my day job while juggling the various social justice pro-bono commitments. Which included presenting a workshop to Local Government Lawyers with the head of Equality, Diversity and Inclusion on my journey, on the significance of the need for diversity within the law; presenting a workshop on "Windrush and Politics 1944–1970" at the National Education Union Conference; and providing training to local councillors on the WCS, alongside many others. I also entered the world of public and motivational presentations on women in the workplace, which included the Law Society of Scotland, various schools, councils and libraries, black workers groups, and the Oxford Alumni Oriel College.

But it wasn't just about my work, it was also about how far I could take it. I felt it necessary to think outside the box, to aspire to new levels. I was an avid reader of the *New Law Journal,* a British weekly magazine for legal professionals, first published in 1822, providing information on case law, legislation, and changes in practice. I'd read the publication for years, noting important articles that tweaked my interest. But in 2023, I decided to take a more active role within the journal. I was a little nervous because although previously I had sent pieces to the *Law Society Gazette* opinions page, I had not had any article featured officially in a legal magazine. But I had something to say, and it was not enough to do it from podiums or workshops. In addition, the *New Law*

Journal is a highly reputable legal publication, so getting an article published within it would be a great achievement for me.

With their submission criteria firmly on board, I pitched my idea, which related to the lack of social mobility within the legal world, with facts and figures about top law firms lacking innovation within exclusive recruitment practices, headhunting graduates from elite backgrounds, and how those from State schools were being overlooked, irrespective of their abilities.

I was ecstatic when the magazine responded with a yes. There were tight timelines and a strict word count, but in May 2023, my article "Time to Pick Up Pace on Social Mobility?"[2] was published. Seeing my work in print was wonderful, mainly as I was writing about something that meant so much to me. What made it even more significant was following postings on my LinkedIn by professionals, and not just from the legal world, who connected with me and provided their thoughts, developing a meaningful conversation.

This illustrated the benefit of sharing my work on a broader platform, opening the way for discussions on the importance of pushing for change. I have since had two further articles published in the *New Law Journal,* "Windrush and the Legacy of Patriots,"[3] celebrating the 75th anniversary of the Windrush Generation arriving in Britain, and "The Dissolution of the Courts,"[4] which considered the devastating effect hundreds of court closures have had on the vulnerable victims caught up within the legal system.

I have morphed myself into a multifaceted social justice champion, on the one hand working with legal, educational, and corporate organizations, speaking truth to power about my own experiences inside and outside the legal world, and the importance of Equality, Diversity and Inclusion strategies, and on the other the wide range of work undertaken in respect of Windrush. However in the Autumn of 2023, I received a call that would introduce me into a celebrity world, that I had not expected.

---

2. Campbell, Pauline, *New Law Journal,* 5 May 2023.
3. Campbell, Pauline, *New Law Journal,* 16 June 2023.
4. Campbell, Pauline, *New Law Journal,* 27 October 2023.

CHAPTER 22

Justice4Windrush and Looking Forward

I t was a Thursday evening; I had been working since seven that morning. It had been a hectic week, and frankly, when my phone rang, I was a little apprehensive about taking it because all I wanted to do was shower and collapse into bed. But I decided to answer; in doing so, a man called Colin McFarlane stated that he had been provided with my details by a mutual friend, who I had spoken to a few days before, and given my permission for my number to be passed on.

Sometimes, you are part of a conversation you will never forget; my first conversation with Colin McFarlane comes squarely within that criterion. Colin is a successful actor who, like myself, is first generation of Windrush parents from Jamaica, who settled and made a home for themselves in Britain. He had an enthusiasm I wanted to bottle as he told me about his campaign, Justice4Windrush, in which he worked with multi-platinum award winner Annie Lennox, one of the most successful female British artists in UK music history. The campaign aimed to bring the plight of those affected by the Windrush Scandal into the mainstream because, despite everything, few people within the British public knew anything about it.

Colin explained how he and Annie wanted to convey the travesty of a situation that had grown stagnant, leaving thousands of black British citizens in limbo. The aim was to bring the great and the good from the music industry, theatre, film, and the legal profession together to get the message out there to as many people across society as possible. That was the beginning of my journey with Colin McFarlane.

Colin was like a whirlwind, with various professionals around him dealing with publicity, legal information, and celebrities, culminating in two days of filming at the Holborn Studios. The Justice4Windrush Campaign was filmed in preparation for its launch, that took place in January 2024, which consisted of celebrities, Windrush victims, and his legal team holding up a sign in front of us with the word "Why?" to the backdrop of Annie Lennox's version of the song. It was a potent day and quite daunting because I felt a little outside my comfort zone, but I was made to feel so welcome I was soon at ease. It's hard to say how quickly things have moved with the campaign, but within just a few months, I worked closely with Colin, dealing with victims and working on various legal documents as the legal adviser to the Justice4Windrush Campaign. For Colin, no job is too big or too small, and like me, he fits all this into his busy schedule as a successful actor.

One particular Saturday night, I had been speaking to Colin well into the early hours. At the end of the conversation, I was shattered and fell asleep with the TV on in the background. Then, between the world of reality and sleep, I heard Colin's voice, but as I opened my eyes, I saw that he was on TV, acting alongside Liam Neeson in the film *The Commuter*.[1] When I spoke to him the following day, we laughed about it, but what this highlighted to me was when it comes to social justice and the importance of voices being heard, one size does not fit all because those of us who believe in it come from every aspect of life. Each voice is equally important. However, Colin understood that to grip society's interest in the Windrush Scandal, he needed to enlist the help of celebrities, who would grab the media's attention.

What I love about Colin's spirit is that there are no boundaries; although I have managed to find my voice and use it, I cannot ignore that the lawyer in me is still prone at times to be on the side of caution. But Colin is fearless; if he wants something to happen, it will. And he will pull out all the stops until it becomes a reality. Perhaps the best example of this is securing free legal advice for Windrush victims, after Brenda King, a leader in driving impactful change across various sectors, arranged a meeting between Justice4Windrush and Clifford Chance, one of the top British law firms in the UK and a member of the "Magic Circle". We spent months discussing matters with the firm to bring them on board as advisers providing support and helping Windrush victims through the application process, which will be led by Justice4Windrush. As the supervising pro bono lawyer for Justice4Windrush, I will be responsible for training them on the history of the Windrush Generation in Britain, the

---

1. "The Commuter," Director Jaume Collet Serra, StudioCanal, Lionsgate Films, 19 January 2018.

importance of understanding their journey, and talking them through the application process.

The first time I met with Clifford Chance, it was a little daunting because, as a public sector lawyer, I was far removed from the corporate world of the massive legal firm. Still, I watched Colin at work; his confidence and ability to champion the short, and long-term goals of Justice4Windrush were terrific. When Colin handed over the reins to me during the meeting to deal with the legal aspects, I was proud to be the voice for the victims from a legal perspective.

In May 2024, Colin attended the "Sheffield Stories: Caribbean Footsteps," Weston Park Museum, an exhibition celebrating the stories of Sheffield and the African Caribbean community. Caribbean Footprints includes photographs, film, and mementos from those who called that city their home after arriving on HMT *Windrush* in 1948. A spokesperson said it is a tribute to how the black community has contributed to life in the city. Exhibits included a cricket bat (1968) signed by young people and organizers living in Sheffield. Simon Jones, one of the community co-curators behind the exhibition, said: "The exhibition stands as a tribute to the enduring resilience, unwavering strength, and rich cultural vibrancy of the African Caribbean community in Sheffield." Notably, the exhibition also features the Justice4Windrush campaign, showing the two films contributed by Justice4Windrush. The exhibition will run for three years, from 10 May 2024 to 2 May 2027. I was so proud when Colin attended the opening of such a significant event. It showed the Caribbean and African journey within the UK and highlighted that we truly have made a home for ourselves and have culturally enriched this country. Within that, the Justice-4Windrush campaign being shown is a stark reminder of the difficulties the black community continues to face, but behind that (and as shown within the two campaign films), people can see how, as a community, black and white people are coming together in the fight for social justice in response to a scandal that has and continues to destroy people's lives.

These, indeed, are exciting times.

The Justice4Windrush campaign continues to go from strength to strength. Still, I can never forget that this campaign, no matter how significant, is part of a well-oiled machine made up of millions of people worldwide who continue to fight for equality and the right to justice every day. The role I play within it is crucial and more fulfilling than I could have imagined.

In April 2024, I was interviewed on Trevor D Sterling's U-Triumph podcast, a series exploring the triumphs and tribulations of extraordinary leaders from diverse backgrounds. Trevor hopes to inspire success by highlighting that irrespective of social background or personal characteristics, with fair opportunity and the appropriate mindset, ultimately, anyone can be successful. I had followed Trevor's achievements for some time, one of only 90 black senior partners in the UK and head of Moore Barlow's award-winning Trauma Service (winner of the UK Diversity Legal Awards Lawyer of the Year in 2019). Trevor is also the chair of the Mary Seacole Trust, having succeeded Lord Soley and received several accolades during his esteemed career. During the podcast, I shared anecdotes of my dual British and Jamaican background and the ups and downs of being a black female lawyer. The time flew by as we laughed and embraced the various achievements throughout our professional and personal lives, with my work with Justice4Windrush being highlighted.

When it was over, I was quite sad because I'd enjoyed speaking to Trevor, who has a way of getting the best out of his interviewees. When the podcast was released a few weeks later, I had to pinch myself that the person speaking to Trevor was the same 15-year-old who, for years, believed a teacher who had told her she was not A-Level material. I wanted to go back and apologise to her for hiding myself and my voice for so long. But I knew I couldn't go back; I could only go forward. Trevor's podcast aims to help those coming behind us to home in on their talents and inner beliefs, irrespective of their background. What we also have to do is all work together to ensure that we do everything we can to push for fairer opportunities, so when our young people begin their journey, they can channel everything they have into being the best they can be. Without the need to break down walls of prejudice.

Hopefully, those of us who have walked that road before them have helped to make that journey a smoother ride, in which they look in the mirror and not only like what they see but love who and everything they have the potential to become.

Postscript

Since I began writing *Lefty Lawyer* the world has moved rapidly on, and the surrounding issues have become even more high profile. My own journey has also progressed at a fast pace in alignment. Accolades have given me not only a stronger belief in myself, but have acted as a catalyst for others who dare to "live the dream," allowing them not to be defined by how others see them, but how they see themselves.

Reaching the coveted shortlist of the Women and Diversity in Law Awards in 2024 was welcome because it highlighted the importance of the representation of women like myself, with our rich cultural mix, within the legal profession. To be recognised for the work I do has been a fantastic honour.

When I was contacted by award winning writer and journalist Kim Willis, wanting to write a feature on me in *Women and Home* magazine, imposter syndrome reared its head, as I considered that I was being asked to tell my story to an iconic publication, with over 350,000 subscribers. Sharing my story with Kim, made it clear that as *women* we need to be celebrated through publications that give us a platform. I took a copy for Mum and she cried as she read Kim's words and looked at the pictures. I was elated when it led to a fuller piece in *Women's Own*, one of the most popular women's magazines in the UK.

In May 2024, I made the "final cut" when I was shortlisted for the Law Society's Legal Hero Awards, a celebration recognising solicitors who've made a positive difference to other people's lives and communities, while also bringing distinction to the legal profession. Hundreds applied so to reach the last group of amazing lawyers was hard to take in. The winners were to be announced at a lunch held in the splendour of the Law Society's Hall in Chancery Lane. Due to imminent court deadlines, and meetings as chair of the Race Equality Network, I made the unwise decision to go into work that morning and just take a half day off. But as is so often the case, meetings spilled over and urgent casework resulted in me running half-an-hour late. On arrival the speeches had started, and I sat at my designated table, hot and flustered. I don't know what I expected, all I know is that when the third winner was announced, I turned to my friend who had accompanied me, grabbed her hand, and said, "It's me!"

As I stood at the podium to collect the award, it was hard to think of myself as a hero, but as I talked about my journey, the racism, and the self-doubts I'd shed along the way, I realised that the real heroes were Mum and Dad and those like them that came here all those years ago to give me and my generation the chance of a better life. It was only right that I dedicated my award to them. Winning the award catapulted me into the spotlight in a way I had not expected. My profile was featured in *The Times,* and on release of my story online on the Law Society's LinkedIn page there were a huge number of posts and comments from law students just starting out. Many, like me, had changed their career path, with one solicitor qualifying at the age of 62.

My journey goes from strength-to-strength. But in the midst of my success and empowerment, it's impossible to ignore what can only be described as the lukewarm reception from those in power around the topics of colonialism, racism, and reparations as they continue to rumble on with their impact on the black community. A reluctance highlighted by new Prime Minister, Keir Starmer insisting that he wants to "look forward" rather than have "very long endless discussions about reparations on the past."[1] A perfect example of the lack of a real understanding of "lived experience," which has enabled him (at least for now) to relegate to the past the ripple effects that slavery continues to have on the black community within Britain. A ripple effect that comes in the form of the "inferiority classification" of black people. This has emerged over time to justify the enslavement of millions, taken hold and remains entrenched within the infrastructures and policies rooted within British society.

In re-booting myself, through re-education, and a renewed self-worth, I see that classification as a myth. In order to dispel it, I dream of returning to the classroom as that 15-year-old girl, where alongside hearing of William Wilberforce I learned how 1780s Britain had a black population of at least 20,000, made up of educated black people, lobbyists called Sons of Africa. London-based

---

1. On his way to the 2024 Commonwealth Summit in Samoa. See Courea, Eleni, Mohdin Aamna, "Starmer says he wants to 'look forward' and not talk about slavery reparations," *Guardian,* 23 October 2024.

black men who worked towards the abolition of the slave trade and greater civil rights for black people in Britain.

Beside the suffragettes I would soak up the history of Mary Prince (1788–1833) who I have written about in *Chapter 16,* the first woman to present an anti-slavery petition to Parliament and to publish an autobiography, *The History of Mary Prince: A West Indian Slave.* A book which was a key part of the anti-slavery campaign.

Together with Mozart, my teachers, classmates and I would discuss black composers such as Ignatius Sancho, who issued four collections of compositions entitled *A Theory of Music;* the first composer of African descent to publish music in the European tradition. On his death he was the first black publisher known to have been given an obituary in the British press. I would revel in the historical importance of Pablo Fanque, the first black circus proprietor, born in a Norwich workhouse. His speciality was horsemanship; he owned and trained his own horses, sometimes up to 30 at a time. He even purchased a horse from Queen Victoria. His circus was amongst the most famous of the Victorian age, his shows playing to packed houses for the best part of 30 years.

It would be wonderful to wave a magic wand to recognise that relaying history in this way does not diminish it, or lay guilt at the door of the modern white world. Instead it enriches our history, which I believe is a key element to reparation, in that we change the narrative about how black people are seen, perceived, and treated, which starts and ends with the hearts and minds of everyone living as part of the only race that matters. The human race.

Index

Helena Normanton and the Opening of the Bar to Women

by Judith Bourne

Foreword by Mary Jane Mossman

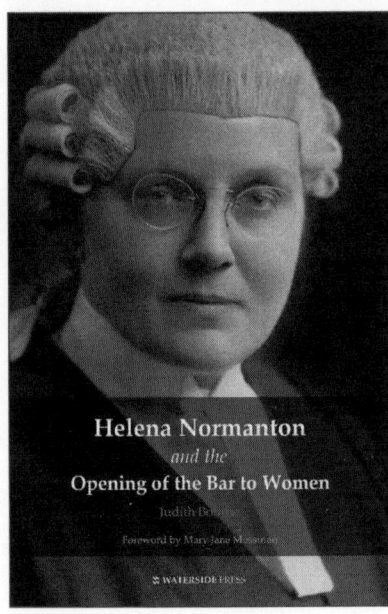

Judith Bourne's acclaimed biography of hitherto little-known lawyer Helena Normanton was published as the campaign for a blue plaque to be placed outside Normanton's home in Mecklenburgh Square, London gained momentum. It tells how, enmeshed in a world of men, she overcame prejudice and discrimination to become one of the first two trailblazing women to join an Inn of Court and practice at the bar of England and Wales.

Paperback & ebook | ISBN 978-1-909976-32-0 | 2016 | 264 pages

www.WatersidePress.co.uk